A STUDY IN THE
THEORY OF ECONOMIC EVOLUTION

CONTRIBUTIONS
TO
ECONOMIC ANALYSIS

III

EDITED BY

J. TINBERGEN
P. J. VERDOORN
H. J. WITTEVEEN

1964
NORTH-HOLLAND PUBLISHING COMPANY
AMSTERDAM

A STUDY IN THE THEORY OF ECONOMIC EVOLUTION

BY

TRYGVE HAAVELMO

1964
NORTH-HOLLAND PUBLISHING COMPANY
AMSTERDAM

First Printing 1954
Second Printing 1956
Third Printing 1964

Printed in the Netherlands

INTRODUCTION TO THE SERIES

This series consists of a number of hitherto unpublished studies, for the greater part by Dutch authors. They are introduced by the editors in the belief that they represent fresh contributions to economic science.

The term *economic analysis* as used in the title of the series has been adopted because it covers both the activities of the theoretical economist and of the research worker.

Although the analytical methods used by the various contributors are not the same, they are nevertheless conditioned by the common origin of their studies, namely theoretical problems encountered in practical research. Since, for this reason, business cycle research and national accounting, research work on behalf of economic policy, and problems of planning are the main sources of the subjects dealt with, they necessarily determine the manner of approach adopted by the authors. Their methods tend to be "practical" in the sense of not being too far remote from application to actual economic conditions. In addition they are quantitative rather than qualitative.

It is the hope of the editors that the publication of these studies will help to stimulate the exchange of scientific information and to reinforce international co-operation in the field of economics.

THE EDITORS

PREFACE

In the Fall of 1949 I gave a short series of lectures at the University of Oslo on the topic of long-range economic tendencies. Subsequently, I have given some more thought to the subject, stimulated by the current actuality of the problem of underdeveloped areas. In the Spring of 1952 I tried to summarize the results of my work in a mimeographed paper entitled: 'Contribution to the Theory of Economic Evolution, with Particular

Reference to the Problem of Backward Areas'. The paper was circulated to a few friends and colleagues, among them Professor J. Tinbergen. He has shown me the great honor and trust of inviting the paper for publication in the present Series. For this purpose I have revised the original mimeographed version to some extent, to improve presentation and to take account of helpful comments received since the paper was first circulated.

The bold choice of a subject as wide and formidable as that of the present monograph would seem to require a foreword with the largest vocabulary of apologies that one could muster. But such an effort is not necessary. In fact, it would be arrogant. Every reader knows the complexity of the subject dealt with well enough not to look for great discoveries in the chapters that follow. If I may mention one thing that I have tried to bring out, it is that the subject of long-range economic development deserves the attention of economic theorists as much as does the worn field of demand curves.

Several of my friends and colleagues have a share in whatever positive fragments there may be in the present study. Professor T. Koopmans has given me constant encouragement to go on with the work. I have had interesting discussions with Mrs. Joan Robinson, N. Kaldor, and R. F. Kahn. My associates at the University Institute of Economics in Oslo, in particular G. Böe, F. Holte, L. Johansen, T. Johnsen, and B. Thalberg, have helped me in various ways with suggestions and by checking the manuscript. I have also received valuable comments from P. Nörregaard-Rasmussen of the University of Copenhagen and from E. Sverdrup of the University of Oslo.

To all those that I have mentioned I owe deep thanks as well as assurances that they should not be blamed for defects of the final product.

Oslo, October 1953   TRYGVE HAAVELMO

TABLE OF CONTENTS

PART IV

THE STOCHASTIC APPROACH

PART V

THEORIES OF INTERREGIONAL RELATIONS

PART VI

SOME SPECULATIONS UPON A
MORE FLEXIBLE THEORETICAL FRAMEWORK

I. INTRODUCTION

1. OBJECTIVES AND POSSIBILITIES OF A THEORY OF EVOLUTIONARY DISSIMILARITIES

In the world economic picture that we can piece together from current international statistics, perhaps the most striking feature is that of *economic dissimilarities*. There are regions where millions of people starve, others where such experiences are long since forgotten; there are regions where productivity is hampered by lack of the most obvious of tools and technological improvements; there are nations where people wade in books and magazines, others where the illiterates are in the majority; there are parts of the world where animals can have better medical attention than people in other areas get.

Faced with all this, should we waste time on lengthy theories that could satisfy our desire for a 'logical explanation'? Is not everything that distracts from immediate and direct material aid a reflection of just plain cynicism? But the answer is not so simple.

First of all, and even if it were pre-determined that we should embark upon a vast program of international, mutual economic aid, there is the problem of how to carry out the program in the most efficient way. Experience from many fields of human activity suggests that it may be efficient not only to plan well for practical operations to be carried out but also to approach the practical problems in a more round-about way, by seeking first to clarify basic principles. And the desire for theoretical groundwork would seem to be the more justified the larger the magnitude of operations to be carried out.

Then there is the — perhaps more fundamental — question of whether theory and research should not probe deeper into the possible long-run consequences of an international parity program. Is it obvious that areas we now call backward would develop economically in a manner similar to that of the economically more advanced countries, provided that sufficient assistance to

1

get started were given? Are we sure that the people in the backward areas want such a development? And—given the opportunity—would they develop into cooperative members of a global economic family, or would they perhaps turn their increasing economic strength into power of agression?

There is probably not much that pure theory can do to answer these fundamental questions. Nor is there much that pure theory can do to help deciding what conclusion regarding aid or non-aid should be drawn from the answers. That is a question of judgment, and the responsibility of decision must rest with the nations and peoples whose future economic and political destiny is involved. But those who have to decide should have access to as much as possible of objective findings of research. Here there is a task of theoretical groundwork.

The ultimate question to be expected from the thinking citizen is as plain as it is scientifically formidable: It is the question *why* certain areas or peoples are economically 'backward' while others are 'advanced'.

Some people may be satisfied by the mere ascertion that economic conditions, skills and habits are 'just different', in the various parts of the world, that people themselves are different, etc. However, if this be the answer, it would at once put any program of economic homogenization in a dubious light. The basic idea underlying all schemes of interregional economic aid and cooperation is no doubt the firm belief that people are essentially alike; that they crave for economic progress in the meaning that this word has in the Western industrialized countries; in other words, that there is something undesirable stopping the people in backward areas from having the same kind of life as the people in—what we call—advanced countries.

Another idea might be that, although people are essentially alike when given equal environments, there are the great differences in natural resources. That is, some people, luckier than others, were born in a land of plenty. However, a little further consideration does not leave too much credit to this 'explanation'. Indeed, it seems next to impossible to think of any measure or index of original, natural resources which is such that all economically advanced countries have much of it while all backward

2

countries have little of it. One might make the explanation a little more flexible by arguing that some people were just lucky to have been born at a time when the global process of economic evolution made the resources of their home land particularly relevant and valuable. But, apart from the dubious explanatory value of this theory, it certainly does not assure us that the countries now in the lead should strive to mold the rest of the world in their own image. There have been many epoques of great material advancement in the course of history, and still their termination, or set-backs, do not today always fill us with sorrow. In order to take actions of aid with confidence and conviction, it would seem necessary to believe that the Western World has now found a path of material progress that points to goals desirable for quite some time to come.

Accepting a more positive point of view, some people might find satisfaction in the belief that all countries are actually on the same path of economic progress but that some of them have not as yet had time to get very far. Taken literally, this theory certainly does not sound reassuring. It is by no means the 'oldest' countries that are the economically more advanced. Of course, if one starts counting time at, say, the beginning of the industrial revolution in Great Britain, the theory may command more credit. However, some peoples and countries have been ahead of others before in history but the ranking has not remained invariant.

There is still another possibility of 'explanation', perhaps somewhat more sophisticated than those above, viz. a theory of the 'wearing-out' of the progressive force, or the resources it feeds on, after a certain long period of advancement. That is, some sort of 'erosion', both literally and in a more figurative sense. But other people would probably like to add the thesis that stagnation of the type indicated is unavoidable only when a society is below a certain level of culture and education. They would hold that more advanced countries should be able to check tendencies towards stagnation by a planned conservation of resources and by scientific alertness.

Now, those are propably some of the ideas in the minds of people whose responsibility it is to direct the international economic policy of their respective countries. And such thoughts

3

are probably also frequently in the mind of the—much larger—groups of people who feel that they are called upon to pay the bill for other peoples' progress. It would seem then that efforts of scientific research in this field would not lack public interest.

But, even if the problems of economic development had been more remote from the public discussion than is the case today, the facts we have before us in this field are perplexing enough to arouse the scientific curiosity of every social scientist. Here we have phenomena like that of neighboring countries whose standards of living have remained at strikingly different levels for centuries. We have countries where income per head has doubled or trippled during the last hundred years while in others there has been only slight progress, or stagnation. And yet, there are probably not as many pages of modern economic theory available on these mysteries as there are books analysing short-run equilibria, or the 'catastrophies' of ten per cent dents in the national income of the more advanced, industrialized countries. The bold and imaginative speculations of the early masters of economic theory upon the broad question of general economic progress have, at least until recently, born comparatively little fruit in the form of modern analytical refinements. [1]

Scientific progress, it is true, should be made wherever one sees an opportunity of discoveries. Experience seems to show that also the demand for practical results is best served when science chooses its own paths. But if a sense of proportions plays a rôle in the choice of topics for scientific efforts, one cannot but wonder why social scientists, and economists in particular, seem to have had a preference for choosing the phenomena of big dissimilarities, the 'real mysteries' of economic life, as the *data* of their theories, while other phenomena, which from a macro-cosmic point of view are only small ripples of variation, are given the most careful 'explanation'.

[1] The rapidly expanding literature in the 'Theory of economic growth' indicates, however, that a real revival of interest in long-range theories is in the making. An illuminating survey of current work in the theory of economic growth is found in Evsey Domar's paper on 'Economic Growth: An Econometric Approach', in *Papers and Proceedings of the Sixty-fourth Annual Meeting of the American Economic Association* (American Economic Review, May, 1952), pp. 479–495. This paper is also a good starting point for references to recent literature in the field.

The common argument in favor of restricting the problems of economic research by ceteris paribus clauses of the type 'given social institutions', 'in the short run', 'constant technique', etc., has been that one wants to study and to test the 'laws of pure economic theory'. But what are the results of efforts in this direction so far?

Let us take the study of demand functions. We have a well developed theory based on the assumption of stable and consistent indifference maps. But when applied to data from a market that we think is comparable with our model, the results of prediction are generally poor. It is true that differences between calculated and actual quantities may not be very large, in absolute terms. But the actual variations are themselves usually rather small, so that we have difficulties in judging whether our theories have brought us beyond the simple fact that in the short run and 'under given conditions' demand is relatively stable.

As another example, consider econometric research upon production functions. We want to find the effects upon output of changes in the factors of production. But our 'purely economic' theories are built to fit a market where, if all the assumptions we make are approximately true, there should not in any case be very significant changes in input and output. The variations that we observe in such a market are mostly the results of the market failing to satisfy exactly the assumptions of the theory! How could we expect to verify a theory from such data? In the field of production we have another type of variation that is significant beyond questioning, viz. the tremendous range in the size of firms, but this phenomenon the economist usually groups under 'social institutions'.

I would venture the guess that there is really a much better chance of significant econometric results if we turn to theories that have as their objects of explanation the really big dissimilarities in economic life. Thus, if we have, side-by-side, two large economic regions of which one has a per capita national product several times as big as the other, there must be a tremendous — and therefore presumably detectable — difference in the 'causal factors' at work in the two cases.

A bird's-eye view of economic life and its history in the various

5

parts of the world shows us three types of really significant economic dissimilarities. One is the economic inequalities as between individuals within any large economic region. Another is — at least for some regions or nations — the tremendous difference in riches as between the present and a sufficiently distant past. A third type of significant dissimilarity is that between the various regions at a given point in time.

The dissimilarity as between individuals of a group is probably not so astonishing, at least not to a statistician. From experiences in biology, psychometry etc., he would here expect to find distributions with a characteristic spread, rather than similarity. But the two other types of dissimilarities are usually measured in terms of *averages* based on a large number of units of observation, i.e. averages, which from a statistical point of view are significantly different beyond doubt. Here we can hardly avoid asking for 'explanation' in the form of a theoretical model capable of producing dissimilarities of the type observed.

It is seen that the problem of 'explanation' can be posed in any one of the following ways: 1) Why is it that particular economic regions have become economically 'advanced' as compared to others? 2) Why is it that certain regions have failed to become economically 'advanced'? 3) How could an 'underdeveloped' area become economically 'advanced'? The general theoretical objective would seem to be an analytical framework capable of producing alternative paths of long-range economic development in a given economic region, and of showing under what conditions a particular alternative will materialize.

Faced with a problem of this magnitude, it would be necessary to apologize for modesty of contributions, even if they went far beyond anything found in the following sections of this study.

2. DOCTRINES OF ECONOMIC EVOLUTION

We have said that theories regarding the nature of long-range economic developments are, relatively, not abundant in the economic literature. But it seems that this statement is truer today than it would have been e.g. in the 18th or the 19th century. The early masters of economic theory were, in fact, intensely interested in the general determinants of economic progress and the broad conditions of wealth or poverty. The title 'An Inquiry into the Nature and Causes of the Wealth of Nations' would not have been chosen by one who thought that the price mechanism in a short-run commodity market was the essence of economics.

Adam Smith reached down to the fundamental factors that spell riches or poverty for a particular nation: The degree of division of labor and the process of capital accumulation. He had a great many things to say—in the form of description—of how these economic factors have developed in the various countries. Another question is, however, to what extent such a description can satisfy our demand for 'explanation'. It is, of course, evident that the original natural riches of a region must have played a great rôle, in particular as long as the international division of labor through international trade was not well developed. It is also clear that racial differences, differences in climate etc. cannot be neglected. But Adam Smith, and subsequently many others, seem to ascribe a considerable part of the interregional economic dis-similarities to conditions that are essentially man-made, such as traditions, form of government, the prevailing general attitude towards free enterprise and commerce, towards rural versus urban development, and so forth. These man-made differences are some-what harder to accept as explanatory factors. In fact, if all people want material progress, the mystery to be explained is precisely why certain groups of people have chosen the road to expansion while others have not. Adam Smith has a remark on China which may indicate his way of thinking in this matter. In Chapter VIII on the wages of labor he writes (p. 71) [1]: 'China has been long one of the richest, that is, one of the most fertile, best cultivated, most industrious, and most populous countries in the world. It seems, however, to have been long stationary. Marco Polo, who visited it more than five hundred years ago, describes its cultivation, industry, and populousness, almost in the same terms in which they are described by travellers in the present times. It had perhaps, even long before his time, acquired that full complement

[1] References to 'The Wealth of Nations' are from The Modern Library edition, New York 1937. (Quoted with the kind permission of the publishers, Random House, Inc., New York.)

of riches which the nature of its laws and institutions permits it to acquire.' And on p. 95: 'But this complement may be much inferior to what, with other laws and institutions, the nature of its soil, climate, and situation might admit of.' Evidently the Chinese had been unwise not to change their laws and institutions! But would — or could — they have done so if they had been told? Or did they already have too heavy a load of cumulated history to be able to dig themselves out? Adam Smith has a passage, in another connection, that may in fact contain an admissible theory of economic growth. Discussing the causes of the prosperity of new colonies he writes (p. 531–532): 'The colony of a civilized nation which takes possession either of a waste country, or of one so thinly inhabited, that the natives easily give place to the new settlers, advances more rapidly to wealth and greatness than any other human society.

'The colonists carry out with them a knowledge of agriculture, and of other useful arts, superior to what can grow up of its own accord in the course of many centuries among savage and barbarous nations.'

Could one also construe this to mean that if a nation is stagnant at a certain level of wealth and culture and if some of its people were then transplanted to a region with more elbowroom, it would mean a release of potential powers of progress? If so, the quotation above contains fragments of an interesting dynamic theory of economic evolution.

No student sincerely interested in long-range economic dynamics could bypass the fundamental contribution of *Malthus*. It is almost inconceivable how writers up to the present day have been able to reduce his brilliant example of stringent, abstract reasoning to that of a cheap prognosis that population would increase in geometric progression! To those who may still adhere to such an interpretation one could probably give no better advice than to study Knut Wicksell's convincing evaluation of the Malthusian theory [1].

The part of Malthus' theory which is of particular interest in the study of long-range economic developments can probably be

[1] Knut Wicksell, Vorlesungen über Nationalökonomie, Erster Band. Jena 1913. Pp. 38–49.

8

summarized as follows: The potential rate of increase of a nation's population probably exceeds by far the rate of increase in the means of subsistence that the population could produce if it were growing at the maximum rate. Hence, population cannot grow continually at its maximum rate. But the propensity to procreate is very strong. The rate of growth of population may, therefore, very well be so high that production per capita remains low or even stationary at the subsistence level. Whether or not this shall be the case depends essentially on the ability to plan for the future that the individuals possess, and that again depends, at least in part, on the actual level of material economic welfare.

One could say that this theory does not go very far in explaining how it came about that certain countries are in a state of economic poverty, coupled with a high birth rate, a high mortality rate and a slowly growing population, while others show a rapid growth both in population and in the per capita income. But the theory does suggest part of an explanation of why a nation, once in the former of the two groups, cannot very easily get on to the road of economic progress by its own power.

The *classical economists* made the Malthusian theory a cornerstone of their theories of long-range economic development. [1] They seem to have had their attention directed in particular toward the possibilities of economic stagnation, arguing that there were strong forces working in this direction in all societies.

Using a somewhat modernized terminology, their model framework could probably be represented as follows:

Let X denote the total annual production in a society, K the total volume of capital, and N the available manpower (which we shall assume is proportional to total population). Assume now, as an illustration, that the 'production function' has the form

$$X = AN^\alpha K^\beta \qquad (2.1)$$

where $\alpha > 0$, $\beta > 0$, $\alpha + \beta < 1$, because of the constancy (or gradual exhaustion) of original natural resources, such as acreage, ore deposits etc.

Suppose further, that X is divided into two shares: That of

[1] Cf. Paul Sweezy, The Theory of Capitalist Development, London 1946, pp. 92–93.

9

labor, which is all consumed, and that of the 'capitalists' (*including landowners*), which is accumulated (apart, perhaps, from a relatively constant amount that the capitalists consume). Suppose that the wage rate w is determined by the marginal productivity of labor, i.e.

$$w = \frac{\partial X}{\partial N} = A a N^{a-1} K^\beta = a \frac{X}{N}. \tag{2.2}$$

The amount of total profits, π, (including rent) is therefore given by

$$\pi = X - w N = (1-a) X. \tag{2.3}$$

Now, if we assume, for simplicity, that all profits are accumulated, we have

$$\dot{K} = \pi = (1-a) X > 0, \tag{2.4}$$

for every positive value of X.

Suppose now that, as long as the wage level is above a certain minimum, $\overline{w}$, population tends to grow very rapidly and that this tendency is sufficient to keep wages approximately at the constant level $\overline{w}$. Then the only 'progress' as far as the conditions of the workers are concerned is that their number grows. An increasing K gives room for more and more workers living at the subsistence level of wages $\overline{w}$. The total amount of profits, π, and, therefore, $\dot{K}$, will increase, but less than in proportion to the amount of capital K. This is seen as follows.

We have, using $N = (aX/\overline{w})$,

$$X = A N^a K^\beta = A \left(\frac{aX}{\overline{w}} \right)^a K^\beta,$$

or

$$X = \left[A \left(\frac{a}{\overline{w}} \right)^a K^\beta \right]^{\frac{1}{1-a}}.$$

The ratio of total profits to capital is, therefore,

$$\frac{\pi}{K} = \frac{(1-a)X}{K} = (1-a) \left[A \left(\frac{a}{\overline{w}} \right)^a \right]^{\frac{1}{1-a}} K^{\left(\frac{\beta}{1-a} - 1 \right)}. \tag{2.5}$$

If, instead of total profits, we consider only that part of π

10

which corresponds to the marginal return on capital, we should have

$$\frac{\partial X}{\partial K} K = \beta X = \frac{\beta}{1-a}\pi.$$

Apart form a positive factor of proportionality, the profit ratio based on this narrower concept of profits would be exactly similar to that given by (2. 5).

Hence, regardless of which of the two profit concepts we look at, the corresponding *rate of profits* will be a function of K which *decreases when K increases, provided $a + \beta < 1$.*

This tendency to a falling rate of profits was thought of as the cause of a gradual reduction and eventual stagnation of the rate of accumulation. However, according to the model above such a tendency could not materialize. Accumulation must go on at an increasing rate no matter how low the rate of profits becomes. To get the aledged tendency towards stagnation some new assumption would have to be introduced, for example the assumption that the capitalists could find alternative uses for their profits, e.g. increased consumption or 'unproductive' accumulation, or the particular, classical, idea of excluding substitution between N and K.

Suppose, next, that the increase in population is not strong enough to keep wages at the subsistence level, or suppose that the working classes would deliberately hold down their rate of reproduction. Then the level of wages as determined by the system above could increase as the accumulation of capital gradually increases the marginal productivity of a given quantity of labor. Suppose for example that N were kept nearly constant, equal to $\bar{N}$, say. Then w would increase with K in the following manner:

$$w = aA\bar{N}^{(a-1)}K^{\beta}, 0 < \beta < 1, \tag{2. 6}$$

while the ratio of profits to capital would fall as K increases, according to the formula

$$\frac{\pi}{K} = (1-a)A\bar{N}^{a}K^{\beta-1}, 0 < \beta < 1. \tag{2. 7}$$

The accumulation of capital would still continue indefinitely, and at an increasing rate.

Thus, if population does not increase too fast, there need be no tendency toward stagnation in the level of wages, or in incomes in

11

general, in the society even if it operates under a general 'law of decreasing return.'

Differences in development as between different nations could be explained by differences in their production functions such as the obvious difference in the 'scale coefficient' A. One could perhaps also think of the possibility that certain nations, because of more natural riches, have had a longer time in relative plenty during which to acquire an understanding of the necessity of population constraints than other less fortunate nations who 'got poor before they got wise.'

The efforts of *Karl Marx* to reach an integrated theory of economic and social evolution surpassed in ambition anything that had been attempted by the classical economists. It is always dangerous, it seems, to try to sum up what Marx's contributions were, because at the moment one thinks that one has got hold of the analytical framework of his ideas, there is another chapter of his massive writings that gives other ideas. And if one does not discover this by ones own efforts, there are enough experts on Marxian theory to scare any outsider from making comments. We could probably do no better for our purpose here than to rely on the judgment of one of the foremost experts in the field, Professor Schumpeter. The following quotation is probably as good a description as any of the Marxian building, if it is to be given in a few sentences [1]:

'I said a moment ago that Marx's synthesis embraces all those historical events — such as wars, revolutions, legislative changes — and all those social institutions — such as property, contractual relations, forms of government — that non-Marxian economists are wont to treat as disturbing factors or as data, which means that they do not propose to explain them but only to analyze their *modi operandi* and consequences.... The trait peculiar to the Marxian system is that it subjects those historical events and social institutions themselves to the explanatory process of economic analysis or, to use the technical lingo, that it treats them not as data but as variables.'

[1] J. A. Schumpeter: Capitalism, Socialism and Democracy. New York 1942. p. 47. (Quoted with the kind permission of the publisher, Harper & Brothers, New York.)

This broader view upon what should be the objects of a general inquiry is certainly a necessary condition for any progress in the field of general economic evolution. But it is of course not enough to get hold of an overwhelming number of new variables. And I think it is fair to say that Marx is more helpful in that direction than he is in comforting an earth-bound model builder who wants the problems boiled down to manageable essentials.

Among the Marxian doctrines particularly relevant to our purpose here is the thesis commonly described as 'the materialistic interpretation of history', that is, if we take the liberty of a somewhat 'dry' specification. To be bold, we could think of this thesis as the foundation of a dynamic theory of economic evolution of the following nature: Economic institutions, as far as they are man-made, and the material results that they produce, are subject to changes, the driving forces of which are themselves outgrowths of the prevailing economic and social system. But why then the big dissimilarities, in this respect, as between the various regions of the world? This question does not necessarily discredit the theory, but it means that we are no closer to the answer to our problem of dissimilarities, unless the process *in time* that the theory suggests can be coupled with a process *in space* showing why certain things should happen here, others there. Thus, even though we may have before us a fruitful basis for a theory, we certainly do not have a complete model in analytical form.

Schumpeter's theory of economic development [1] is, if not in method at least in scope, an outgrowth of Marxian and Neo-Marxian thinking. Schumpeter's theory of economic evolution, though it embraces a much wider group of phenomena than that which 'pure economics' usually reckons as its 'quaesita', is, nevertheless, somewhat less ambitious than a desire to rewrite the whole history of economic and social life. Schumpeter is looking for the driving forces in the process of capitalistic economic development, and he finds his answer in the concept of innovations. The question is then whether we are satisfied with an 'explanation' that makes use of innovations as an external force, or whether we want to think of the innovations as only one of several ways in which the

[1] J. A. Schumpeter: The Theory of Economic Development. Harvard University Press. 1949.

perpetual human struggle for progressive changes manifests itself. We are in any case far from an explanation of how these forces could operate with such obviously different results in the various parts of the globe.

More recent studies in the theory of long-range development have on the whole been somewhat less spectacular in scope than those reviewed above. This fact may be due, in part, to an — in itself admirable — desire for greater analytical clarity. But in part it is no doubt also a result of the drive towards scientific special- ization which has resulted in dividing social science up into sepa- rate compartments: Economics, Sociology, Demography, etc.. However, the current interest in the problems of underdeveloped areas as well as in economic and social development in general is turning this trend. The 'heavy' parameters, such as Population, Capital, and Technology, are reoccupying their place as important endogenous variables of economic theory. [1]

Formidable efforts of quantitative research have been made by *Collin Clark*[2]. His contribution towards rational classification and measurement of the objective criteria of economic progress is unquestionably a significant step in the direction of an econometric approach. We reserve the next section for further comments on the importance of settling such problems of classification and measure- ment.

3. PROBLEMS OF DESCRIPTION AND MEASUREMENT

We have been discussing the problems of explaining interregional disparities in economic development and we have reviewed some theories of the determinants of economic evolution. But in so doing we have more or less dodged the fundamental issue of how to choose, define and measure relevant descriptive characteristics of economic progress. If one were to raise these problems on a really broad basis, it is obvious that one could end rather deep in

[1] A very stimulating piece of reading in this connection is the recently published collection of lectures by Ragnar Nurkse: Some Aspects of Capital Accumulation in Underdeveloped Countries. National Bank of Egypt. Fiftieth Anniversary Commemoration Lectures. Cairo 1952.

[2] Collin Clark, The Conditions of Economic Progress.. Second edition, London, 1951.

the philosophy of what are 'good' things and 'bad' things of life in general. One could very likely justify — or on certain premises, that are not entirely unreasonable, even *prove* — that intertemporal, interregional, interracial, etc., comparisons are meaningless if one aims to answer the question whether and by how much some people feel richer and happier than others.

But we shall have to settle for less than this, if we do not want to lose entirely the contact with more practical problems of international economic policy. In fact, we shall probably not be able to claim more than the following properties of the descriptive characteristics that we choose: 1) They should have a definite meaning in terms of actual or potential observability for all the economic units to which they are applied; and 2) they should be such that, if used for international comparisons, we would get an 'economic ranking' of countries corresponding, roughly, to that which today forms the basis for discussions on international economic policies. This is, admittedly, not a very satisfactory answer from a more philosophical point of view. On the other hand, we have some excuse in the circumstance that we do not want to settle the question whether or not all countries *ought* to be like those that we today call economically advanced. We are merely(!) searching for possible explanations of *why in fact* they are not alike.

There is, however, a definitional question that has to be discussed even before we start specifying variables, viz. the question of the *units* to which the variables apply. We have been speaking rather loosely about 'countries', 'economic areas', 'regions' etc.. In some cases existing political borderlines between countries are relevant lines of demarcation for the purpose of economic comparisons. In other cases this is not so. A purely geographical subdivision has the advantage that it is historically invariant, but such areas would not necessarily form natural units from the point of view of e.g. demographic criteria or of political affiliations. The best we can do from the point of view of pure analytical theory is probably simply to postulate the existence of a *network of economic* regions well-defined at any point of time and having economic properties described implicitly by the model economic structure ascribed to them. It may be possible to include as a part of the model structure, certain types of changes in the regional

15

network itself. One would, of course, like to choose models directly applicable to available facts. On the other hand, it is very often the case that one does not even know what interesting facts to look for before one has a model framework in which to interpret them.

The problem of a meaningful definition of an economic region is closely tied to another general problem that will bother us: the ever-present problem of *aggregation*. In order to give meaning to aggregate economic variables one would usually require that the group (of people, households, firms etc.) to which the aggregates apply should in some sense consist of 'economically similar' units. The importance of this requirement depends to some extent, however, upon the nature of the theory one has in mind, that is, whether one has a theory where the economic decisions and actions are ascribed to single individuals and other small, 'natural' decision units, or whether the behavioristic elements of the theory are meant to apply directly to larger groups *as such*.

If the individuals, the single firms etc. are considered the only 'natural' economic units, one could perhaps say that the problem of aggregation is only a formal problem that arises whenever, for some reason, we want to group the basic units. We would be free to consider any grouping that might interest us. But if we choose a more 'collectivistic' point of view with regard to macro-economic theories, that is, if we want to take the attitude that 'the whole' may in many respects be something more than, or quite different from, 'the sum of the parts', the choice of groups becomes all important. At the same time one could probably argue that a 'natural' grouping is automatically provided by the political and geographic subdivision of people into 'nations', because of a high correlation between geographic proximity, political unity and common economic interests.

One may have likes or dislikes for any one of the two interpretations of macro-economic theory we have mentioned. But there is certainly as yet very little empirical evidence to show that one of them is 'correct' and the other is 'false'. One should therefore feel free to use either one of them, and judge them by the results of application for descriptive and explanatory purposes.

What specific *aggregate* criteria would be relevant as indicators of general economic prosperity? Among the things that we usually associate with prosperity are undoubtedly the following:

High level of per capita production, large amounts of physical capital per head, high standards of general education and technical skill, high average expectation of life. When we say 'high' and 'large' we mean, of course, relatively, in space or time.

If we try to rank the various countries or geographic regions by means of the above-mentioned criteria, we shall find that there are other characteristic dissimilarities, at least between the regions at the extreme ends of the scale. Thus, we shall find very typical differences in birth rates and death rates, both of these being much higher in 'backward' regions than in 'advanced' regions. We shall find that the advanced regions are also on the whole *advancing* faster than the backward regions, in terms of the criteria mentioned. We shall find not only that these facts are different but also that, at least apparently, the propensities of the people towards changing their economic and social environments are far from similar. One could complete this broad picture by loads of more descriptive information in figures and facts.

Can the long list of descriptive characteristics be condensed to something like those that we, tentatively, suggested to use for a ranking of the various regions? If we are to make progress in understanding, on an analytical basis, we have to believe in the possibility of simplification in terms of a few aggregates. By this I do not mean that we should pick out a few aggregate series of production, savings, etc. from statistical yearbooks and disregard all other information. We have to proceed differently: We have to *construct* certain macro-variables, the 'true meaning' of which is given only implicitly by the nature of the theoretical framework in which they are used. A tremendous amount of experience and factual information is used, explicitly or implicitly, consciously or unconsciously, in forging a theoretical model. That is probably why we very often have the strong feeling that the theoretical concepts of a model 'mean something' in terms of facts even if it seems next to impossible to observe and measure exactly what we are thinking of. If we are impatient for explicit results, we tend to choose — though often with grief — a theoretical framework for which it is easy to find 'good corresponding data'. If we have more time a strong conviction of *observability* may satisfy us. In fact, many types of actual observations and measurements would not have been made if they had not been preceded by purely speculative theories.

In view of the relatively sober list of variables that we shall choose to operate with in the present study, the reader may feel that the defensive prologue above uses too heavy ammunition. The list of variables that we think sufficient for our purpose is simply this:

1. Some index of total productive output of a region.
2. The size of the regional population.
3. Some index of the total of accumulated capital.
4. Some index of the level of education and technical knowledge.

One could say that these are, after all, well-known, though troublesome, concepts in current statistics, apart perhaps from item 4, and even for this item there are the statistics on the number of schools, libraries etc. But we should like to warn that we have the intention of 'misusing' the simple terminology of the list above, as compared to its practical content in current statistics. Thus, we shall have occasion to think of 'capital' as some general index of 'productive power' combining the effects of physical accumulation, education and technical know-how. We shall have occasion sometimes to think of 'production' only as a potential source of accumulation and to include in the variable 'production' anything (e.g. exploitation of, or aggression upon, other regions) that could be relevant to the growth of the generalized index of 'capital' as mentioned above. And so forth. This is what we meant when we said earlier that we want to *construct* variables to be used in certain theoretical frameworks. One could say that it would then be better to use other names. However, even in mathematics x does not always mean the same thing!

4. SCRUTINY OF ADMISSIBLE HYPOTHESES

With the conceptual framework outlined in the preceding section as a background we want, briefly, to review some of the ideas upon which a theory of long-range economic development could be built.

We have said that a study of evolutionary dissimilarities between various regions could in a sense be transformed into a study of alternative possibilities of evolution for a given region. In a study of such alternatives the most obvious possibility would seem to be the following: We try to construct a macro-dynamic model the variables of which are the fundamental characteristics of economic evolution, such as population, the amount of available capital, the level of education and know-how, and the rate of production. A determinate, dynamic system would result in certain timepaths of the variables. These timepaths would, in general, depend on certain behavioristic parameters, certain technological parameters and on a set of 'initial conditions' of the system. If a sufficiently general model of this kind could be constructed, the study of dissimilarities would be reduced to a study of how the timepaths of the variables change when the values of the parameters and the initial conditions are changed.

More specificly, one could think of such a dynamic system as incorporating relations of the following well-known categories:

1) A 'production function', showing how total output is determined by the total available manpower, the amount of capital and the level of general education and know-how. The parameters of such a relation would be partly technological (natural resources, etc.), partly institutional.

2) An 'accumulation function', showing the rate of growth of capital, general education and know-how as a function of current production, total population, and the amounts of capital and general knowledge already accumulated, and involving behavioristic parameters reflecting the intensity of human desires towards a better future'.

3) A 'law of population growth', expressing the relative rate of growth of the population as a function of the 'propensity to procreate', and of the rate of deaths, the latter depending again at least in part on economic conditions. [1]

[1] Interesting ideas in the direction of more comprehensive models are found in W. W. Rostow's recent book on 'The Process of Economic Growth', New York, 1952. (See in particular pp. 69–70). This book may serve as an

Each of these relations might be specified in various ways, they might be split up into several functions by considering sub-aggregates etc. In part II we shall study several explicit models of the type indicated.

Suppose now that, by appropriate choice of the parameters involved in the system, the resulting timepaths of production, of population growth, etc., could be made to fit the evolutionary history of any region. Would this be a satisfactory theory of dissimilarities? One could probably agree that the dynamic model would serve a very useful purpose in facilitating the classification of the various types of evolutionary processes.

A more difficult point is the following. If, in setting up a model, we have really succeeded in getting down to fundamentals, most of us would probably like to think that the parameters which so to speak describe human nature ought to be rather much alike, if not identical, for the various regional populations we compare. That would leave only technological parameters, institutional parameters and 'initial conditions' that could be different as between the various regions. In fact, as the parameters we usually call 'technical' and 'institutional' are also to a large extent man-made, there would be still fewer things to be considered as a source of basic dissimilarities.

If one wants to rely chiefly on differences in initial conditions to explain evolutionary dissimilarities, the consequence is that one must think in terms of dynamic systems where initial conditions have a really decisive influence upon the resulting evolutionary process, e.g. such that certain initial conditions may lead to secular stagnation while others do not. (Otherwise, we know that there are factual processes of economic evolution which the system could not cover.) In part II we shall consider certain non-linear systems that have this property.

There is, of course, also another possibility. Even if one does not want to consider the various regional populations as basically

important source of reference for model builders in the field of long-range economic developments. Strict requirements of analytical manageability will, however, no doubt imply a considerable reduction in the number of admissible variables and parameters as compared to the large selection which the author brings into his verbal reasonings. Cf. also J. R. Hicks' review of the book in *The Journal of Political Economy*, Vol. LXI, April 1953, pp. 173–174.

different, it is possible that even small differences, in the long run could lead to very big dissimilarities between the levels of riches. Thus, to illustrate, if two persons had the same salary of, say $ 4000 a year and one of them saved $ 1 every year while the other just broke even, we should probably not consider them very different in the matter of thrift. However, if they both lived to the age of Methuselah, and the rate of interest was 5 per cent, say, they should certainly be very differently situated. One could perhaps express the same fact by saying that they would gradually develop into two very different persons.

Another point of view would be that the evolutionary system is subject to random shocks which may gradually be cumulated into very different long-run patterns even if the systems compared were 'in the beginning' rather similar. In Part IV we shall make some efforts to study such possibilities analytically.

Another element is brought into the picture by the fact that we shall have to consider the effects of the co-existence of many, more or less interconnected, regions. The question then presents itself whether the fact that one particular region, perhaps accidentally, has struck a path of progress and growing economic power means that it is expanding at the expense of other regions, or whether, on the contrary, there is some sort of complementarity between progress in the various regions. To the extent that advancement in a particular region is due to new methods or new thinking, there is undoubtedly some effect of *contagion* upon other regions. Whether such effects would tend always to homogenize developments in all regions is another question. Thus, for example, if progress in one region has resulted, e.g. in a certain fashion in consumption and if this was the only contagious part of the development, the adoption of it in other regions might be premature and might in fact hamper their speed of progress. On the whole the element of complementarity between progress in the various regions is probably stronger when it comes to advancement in education and know-how than is the case for the more materialistic part of progress.

Competition for a large share in limited world resources may lead to suppression and exploitation of certain regions. Here there is certainly a considerable difference between the case where an

21

advanced region simply extracts and removes resources from a less developed region and the case where people from the advanced region actually move into and settle in the underdeveloped region.

No matter how one agrees to define the network of regions, a theory aiming at describing their concurrent economic development is bound to become very involved. In fact, a really serious study of long-range evolution in this respect would probably take us far into the dynamics of power politics and the game of coalitions. It is conceivable that modern theories of games of strategy here could serve as an analytical tool e.g. to study whether interregional power politics tends to preserve or to increase economic dissimilarities or whether, on the contrary, such policies might not lead to a leveling out of disparities. In the present study we do not, however, hope to get very far into analyses of this nature even though it is quite possible that the final answer to our problem lies precisely in that direction. In Part V we shall, however, offer a few more thoughts on the subject.

Dynamic models of the type that we have been discussing, even those that admit of 'external influences' in the form of random shocks, have a property which raises a really fundamental philosophical issue, viz. the property of being *deterministic*. Once set in motion they would describe the future path of economic development for every region with fatalistic necessity. This fact is not essentially altered by the introduction of random shocks because, if the shocks are defined as random variables, there is something absolutely predetermined about them too, viz. their stochastic properties.

It may be that the deterministic point of view is actually a very fruitful one. And it is, of course, always possible to choose deterministic schemes — in particular probabilistic ones — that are so general that no amount of experience and observations could prove the scheme to be 'false'. But it may be that our conceptual framework, in particular that of a network of co-existing regions, with concurrent economic dissimilarities as the unknowns to be explained, is not sufficiently general to fit such a deterministic dynamic model. Perhaps the starting point is artificial in that it tends to emphasize too much the problem of *where* progress is taking place or not taking place, rather than the problem of *what*

22

kind of progress is characteristic for each epoque of history, regardless of regional location. One could instead take the point of view that economic evolution is one big, global process, following perhaps some general predetermined pattern, and that the existence and the shifting of regional dissimilarities are rather incidental to the general process.

However, it seems that one could carry the deterministic point of view too far. In fact, speaking somewhat philosophically, it is a question whether it is consistent to put oneself in the position of an autonomous investigator of human behavior and at the same time leaving no autonomy of action and decision with those that are the objects of investigation.

Speaking less in the abstract, it may be that the goal of demonstrating with logical necessity why one region developed economically in this way, another in that way, is far too ambitious. What one can hope to do is perhaps no more than to *register alternative paths* of economic development that are feasible at any point of time and to show how the set of alternatives is restricted by natural conditions and by the economic history of the region up to the time considered. In certain instances one could probably go a little farther, to show how the history of a given region, in particular with regard to its level of education and knowledge, may restrict the set of feasible paths of development that are actually visualized by the people concerned. In Part VI of this study we .shall investigate certain possibilities of inventing an analytical framework that could give room for some ideas of the kind that we have here indicated.

II. SIMPLE MODELS OF ECONOMIC GROWTH

BASIC CONCEPTS

The macrodynamic theories of economic growth studied in the next four sections contain (in one way or another) variables of the following kind:

1. Volume of production (X, x).
2. Size of the population concerned (N).
3a. Accumulated capital (K, k).
3b. Accumulated level of general education and 'know-how' (S).

The third and the fourth group have been marked 3a and 3b, to indicate that, in certain very rudimentary models, we may want to cover both by one single variable, called 'Capital'.

We have previously said that, in order to talk with precision about variables of the above-mentioned type, it is necessary to define 'units' to which the variables are attached. We shall assume that such units have been defined. We shall call them 'economic regions'.

The symbols used for the various variables are indicated in parenthesis under each of the above-mentioned four groups. Further necessary specifications will be taken care of by means of subscripts, superscripts, etc. However, such specifications will only be introduced if they are necessary to distinguish between concepts *within a particular model*. No effort will be made to keep the 'meaning' of a particular symbol invariant from one model to the next. Efforts in this direction often creates a feeling of consistence that is in fact illusory. The theoretical 'meaning' of a particular variable can be given only implicitly, by the mathematical nature of the model into which it enters. And its factual 'meaning' must be indicated in each case by a description of the concrete measurements or observations with which it is hoped that the corresponding theoretical variable may be successfully identified.

The main emphasis in the following discussion of models is upon formal properties. Some of the models are more highly simplified than others, in relation to known facts. If we were looking for a final, 'best', model, some of the simpler ones might have been discarded, except perhaps for their didactic value. However, our main purpose here is not to reach a final, realistic model. As will be shown in Part III, the view that there should exist one particular dynamic model of universal validity is not easy to defend, against the observable facts of evolutionary dissimilarities. Our chief purpose in the following analysis is merely to *examplify conceivable structures* of evolution, and, in particular, to show explicitly how it is possible to produce evolutionary dissimilarities by granting certain, perhaps slight, differences in structural parameters or initial conditions. Certainly, the models considered are by themselves not particularly original. But I have not found elsewhere a sufficiently broad collection of similar models that could serve as a convenient basis for a comparative analysis of the kind dealt with in Part III. This is the main justification for the following technical details.

5. SYSTEMS WITH NO ACCUMULATION

In this section we shall consider some simplified cases where we assume that the variables from groups 3a and 3b above are constants.

5. 1. *A generalization of the 'Logistic Law'* [1]

Let the law of growth of a population of size N be given by

$$\frac{\dot{N}}{N} = a - \beta \frac{N}{X}, \qquad \left(\dot{N} \text{ means } \frac{dN}{dt}\right), \qquad (5.1.1)$$

where a and β are positive constants and where X is the total flow of means of subsistence available to the population. Here a may be interpreted as the rate of births, and $\beta \frac{N}{X}$ as the rate of deaths;

---

[1] Cf. e.g. the article by Silvio Vianelli: A general dynamic geographic scheme and its application to Italy and the United States. *Econometrica*, July, 1936, pp. 269–283.

or, more generally, the rates of births and of deaths may be linear functions of $\frac{N}{X}$ adding up to the expression in the right hand member of (5. 1. 1). $\frac{N}{X}$ is the 'population density' at time t.

If X is a constant independent of t, the law of population growth given by (5. 1. 1) is the ordinary 'logistic'. It is however, a characteristic of human populations that X is a result of 'production' and can be altered by human efforts.

Let the production function of the population be of the simple type

$$X = aN + b, \qquad (5. 1. 2)$$

when a and b are non-negative constants.

Combining (5. 1. 1) and (5. 1. 2) we get the following explicit differential equations:

$$\frac{\dot{N}}{N} = \frac{(aa-\beta)N + ab}{aN + b}, \qquad (5. 1. 3)$$

$$\frac{\dot{X}}{X-b} = \frac{(aa-\beta)X + \beta b}{aX}. \qquad (5. 1. 4)$$

Furthermore, if $x = \frac{X}{N} =$ average 'income', we have for x the following differential equation

$$\frac{\dot{x}}{x-a} = \frac{\beta-ax}{x}. \qquad (5. 1. 5)$$

In the discussion of these equations we may restrict ourselves to cases where the variables N and X remain *positive*. It then follows, from our assumptions, that for all values of t,

$$X > b \qquad (5. 1. 6)$$

$$x > a. \qquad (5. 1. 7)$$

The system has stationary solutions as follows:

$$\overline{N} = \frac{ab}{\beta-aa}, \qquad (5. 1. 8)$$

$$\overline{X} = \frac{\beta b}{\beta-aa}, \qquad (5. 1. 9)$$

$$\overline{x} = \frac{\beta}{a}. \qquad (5. 1. 10)$$

26

An interesting question is now whether these stationary solutions are stable when positive. In order that this be the case it is necessary and sufficient that

$$aa - \beta < 0. \qquad (5.\,1.\,11)$$

The condition is necessary to keep solutions positive. Now suppose that $N < \bar{N}$. Then, from (5.\,1.\,3) we see that $\dot{N} > 0$ when (5.\,1.\,11) holds, that is, N moves towards $\bar{N}$. Similarly, if $N > \bar{N}$, $\dot{N}$ is negative and, hence, N moves towards $\bar{N}$. (5.\,1.\,11) also insures the stability of X. Furthermore, if N moves towards $\bar{N}$ and X towards $\bar{X}$ as t increases, then x moves towards $\bar{x}$.

Suppose that $aa - \beta > 0$. Then, by (5.\,1.\,3), $N(t)$ will increase steadily in such a way that the relative increase $\dfrac{\dot{N}}{N}$ is larger than a certain positive constant for all values of t. But this means that $N \to \infty$ as $t \to \infty$. From (5.\,1.\,2) it is then seen that $x \to a$ as $t \to \infty$.

Thus, if the system is unstable, *'income per head'*, x, *converges towards an asymptote* $x = a$. However, the asymptote $x = a$ is itself not a solution of the system (5.\,1.\,1) and (5.\,1.\,2).

These properties of the model may be studied more directly from the complete solutions of the equations (5.\,1.\,3), (5.\,1.\,4) and (5.\,1.\,5) which are given implicitly by the following expressions, (where C_1, C_2, and C_3 are constants of integration of which one is arbitrary),

$$\frac{\beta}{a(aa-\beta)} \operatorname{Log} \left| (aa-\beta)N + ab \right| + \frac{1}{a} \operatorname{Log} N = t + C_1, \qquad (5.\,1.\,12)$$

$$\frac{\beta}{a(aa-\beta)} \operatorname{Log} \left| (aa-\beta)X + \beta b \right| + \frac{1}{a} \operatorname{Log} (X-b) = t + C_2, \qquad (5.\,1.\,13)$$

$$\frac{1}{aa-\beta} \left(\frac{\beta}{a} \operatorname{Log} \left| ax-\beta \right| - a \operatorname{Log} (x-a) \right) = t + C_3. \qquad (5.\,1.\,14)$$

('Log' means natural logarithms).

The conclusions to be drawn from the model discussed above can be summarized as follows:

(A) Regarding size of population: If the 'growth coefficient' a is sufficiently small, the size of population, N, will approach the positive level $\bar{N}$. This level is the higher the higher is the value

27

of a, as long as $a < \beta/a$. $\overline{N}$ will be the smaller the larger is β. N will then be ascending or descending, depending on whether the initial value of N is smaller than or larger than $\overline{N}$. If $a > \beta/a$, N will grow beyond limits.

(B) Regarding 'volume of production': X is related to N by the linear equation (5. 1. 2). Therefore, similar conclusions as those under (A) apply to X. $\overline{X}$ will be the smaller the larger is β.

(C) Regarding 'average income': If the 'growth coefficient' a is $< \beta/a$, x will approach a level $\overline{x} = \frac{\beta}{a}$, which is the higher the smaller is a. If a is $> \beta/a$, x will be descreasing and will approach its lower limit a. $\overline{x}$ is the higher the larger is β.

5. 2. *An Alternative: Non-linear Production Function*

We shall assume, as before, that

$$\frac{\dot{N}}{N} = a - \beta \frac{N}{X} \qquad (5.\,2.\,1)$$

but that the production function is

$$X = AN^a, \qquad (5.\,2.\,2)$$

where A and a are positive constants.

From (5. 2. 2) it follows that

$$\frac{\dot{X}}{N} = ax \frac{\dot{N}}{N} \qquad (5.\,2.\,3)$$

or, by using (5. 2. 1),

$$\frac{\dot{X}}{N} = aax - a\beta \qquad (5.\,2.\,4)$$

Multiplying (5. 2. 1) by $\frac{X}{N}$ and subtracting the result from (5. 2. 4) we find

$$\dot{x} = a\,(a-1)\,x - \beta\,(a-1), \qquad (5.\,2.\,5)$$

or, if $a \neq 1$,

$$x = \left(x_o - \frac{\beta}{a}\right) e^{a(a-1)t} + \frac{\beta}{a}, \qquad (5.\,2.\,6)$$

where x_0 is an arbitrary constant.

28

From (5. 2. 2) we have $x = AN^{a-1}$, or, if $a \neq 1$, $N = \left(\frac{x}{A}\right)^{\frac{1}{a-1}}$. Using (5. 2. 6) we obtain

$$N = \left[\frac{1}{A}\left(\left(x_o - \frac{\beta}{a}\right)e^{a(a-1)t} + \frac{\beta}{a}\right)\right]^{\frac{1}{a-1}}. \qquad (5. 2. 7)$$

For X we have

$$X = A\left[\frac{1}{A}\left(\left(x_o - \frac{\beta}{a}\right)e^{a(a-1)t} + \frac{\beta}{a}\right)\right]^{\frac{a}{a-1}}. \qquad (5. 2. 8)$$

If $0 < a < 1$, i.e. 'decreasing return', and if $x_o > \frac{\beta}{a}$, x will decrease, approaching $\frac{\beta}{a}$, while N and X will increase, approaching $\overline{N} = \left(\frac{Aa}{\beta}\right)^{\frac{1}{1-a}}$, and $\overline{X} = A\left(\frac{Aa}{\beta}\right)^{\frac{a}{1-a}}$, respectively. If $0 < a < 1$, and $0 < x_o < \frac{\beta}{a}$, x will increase, approaching $\frac{\beta}{a}$, while N and X will decrease, approaching $\overline{N}$ and $\overline{X}$ as above.

If $a > 1$, i.e. 'increasing return', and if $x_o > \frac{\beta}{a}$, x will increase beyond limits, while N and X also increase beyond limits. If $a > 1$ and $x_o < \frac{\beta}{a}$, x, X and N will decrease to zero, which is by assumption a lower limit of the variables considered.

The main difference between the model in 5. 1 and the model in 5. 2 is that in the latter the value of the 'coefficient of productivity', a, determines whether or not the system is stable, regardless of the (positive) values of a and β.

6. MODELS FOR A STATIONARY POPULATION

6. 1. *A Linear Model of Production and Capital Accumulation*

Let X denote production per unit of time and K the existing amount of capital. We shall study the following model:

$$X = A + \varkappa K, \qquad (6. 1. 1)$$

$$\dot{K} = \gamma X + \gamma_o, \qquad (6. 1. 2)$$

Here A, $\varkappa$ and γ are positive constants and γ_o a negative constant.

29

(6. 1. 1) is a 'production function', (6. 1. 2) an accumulation function [1]. The equations are assumed to be valid only for $K \geq 0$.

From the model above it follows that

$$K = (K_o - \bar{K})e^{\gamma \varkappa t} + \bar{K} \qquad (6. 1. 3)$$

$$X = \varkappa (K_o - \bar{K})e^{\gamma \varkappa t} + \varkappa \bar{K} + A \qquad (6. 1. 4)$$

where K_o is an arbitrary constant, and where

$$\bar{K} = -\frac{\gamma A + \gamma_o}{\gamma \varkappa} \qquad (6. 1. 5)$$

If $K_o > \bar{K}$, both K and X will grow beyond limits when $t \rightarrow \infty$. If $K_0 < \bar{K}$, K will reach zero at a finite value of t. X will then at the same time reach the value $X = A$. With $\varkappa$ and γ positive the solution is, therefore, always unstable.

6. 2. *An Alternative Linear Model of Production and Capital Accumulation*

Let the production function be the same as in the preceding model, viz.

$$X = A + \varkappa K. \qquad (6. 2. 1)$$

But assume now that the rate of capital accumulation is influenced directly by the existing amount of capital. This influence may be thought of as the sum of two components, one which is positive

---

[1] One could think of (6. 1. 2) as similar to the propensity to save out of income. However, much controversy has arisen in the economic literature regarding the possibility of measuring 'capital' in such a way that 'income not consumed' equals the rate of growth of capital. When we consider a capital concept as wide as the one visualized here, such a definition becomes even more problematic. It is, of course, formally possible to measure capital in the same units as X, and such that the growth of capital equals a part of X. But the trouble then is whether this concept of capital makes sense when regarded as a *factor of production*. It might at any rate require considering a very awkward form of production function. In addition, it is by no means certain that it is good theory to regard 'consumption' as an *alternative* to accumulation. Even if one does not want to go as far as to regard consumption as 'input', there are undoubtedly certain parts of what we usually call consumption that are more complementary to accumulation than competing with it. On the basis of these considerations we have chosen, in what follows, to regard accumulation as some function of total output, without imposing the additivity requirement that accumulation + consumption = production.

and which reflects the better opportunity of planning for the future when more capital is at hand, and one which is negative, representing some sort of 'saturation' effect. Accordingly, we now write the accumulation function as

$$\dot{K} = \gamma_1 X + \gamma_2 K + \gamma_0, \qquad (6.\,2.\,2)$$

where $\gamma_1 > 0$, $\gamma_0 < 0$, while γ_2 may be either positive or negative, depending on which of the two influences mentioned above is the stronger.

From this model it follows that

$$K = (K_o - \bar{K})e^{(\gamma_1 \varkappa + \gamma_2)t} + \bar{K}, \qquad (6.\,2.\,3)$$

$$X = \varkappa (K_o - \bar{K})e^{(\gamma_1 \varkappa + \gamma_2)t} + \varkappa \bar{K} + A, \qquad (6.\,2.\,4)$$

where K_o is an arbitrary constant and where

$$\bar{K} = -\frac{\gamma_1 A + \gamma_0}{\gamma_1 \varkappa + \gamma_2} \qquad (6.\,2.\,5)$$

If $K_o > \bar{K}$ and $\gamma_1 \varkappa + \gamma_2 > 0$ both K and X will grow beyond limits. If on the other hand γ_2 is negative and sufficiently small, $\gamma_1 \varkappa + \gamma_2$ will be < 0 and K will approach the stationary level $\bar{K}$, while X approaches $A + \varkappa \bar{K}$ (provided that $\bar{K} > 0$).

6.3. *A Non-linear Production Function*

Let us study a model similar to that in 6.2, but with non-linear productivity of capital. A very simple but somewhat artificial model of this kind is

$$(X - a) = bK^\varkappa, \qquad (6.\,3.\,1)$$

$$\dot{K} = \gamma_1 (X - a) + \gamma_2 K, \qquad (6.\,3.\,2)$$

where a, b, $\varkappa$, γ_1, γ_2 are constants. (a is some sort of minimum income produced without capital)

From this model we have

$$\dot{K} = \gamma_1 b K^\varkappa + \gamma_2 K, \qquad (6.\,3.\,3)$$

31

the solution of which is

$$K = \frac{1}{\left[\left(B + \frac{\gamma_1 b}{\gamma_2}\right)e^{(1-\varkappa)\gamma_2 t} - \frac{\gamma_1 b}{\gamma_2}\right]^{\frac{1}{\varkappa-1}}}, \qquad (6.\,3.\,4)$$

where B is an arbitrary constant.

For X we then obtain the solution

$$X = \frac{b}{\left[\left(B + \frac{\gamma_1 b}{\gamma_2}\right)e^{(1-\varkappa)\gamma_2 t} - \frac{\gamma_1 b}{\gamma_2}\right]^{\frac{\varkappa}{\varkappa-1}}} + a. \qquad (6.\,3.\,5)$$

In connection with (6.3.4) we may discuss four different alternatives, viz. 1) $\varkappa < 1$, $\gamma_2 < 0$; 2) $\varkappa < 1$, $\gamma_2 > 0$; 3) $\varkappa > 1$, $\gamma_2 < 0$; 4) $\varkappa > 1$ $\gamma_2 > 0$.

Case 1): $\varkappa < 1$, $\gamma_2 < 0$. If $B > -\frac{\gamma_1 b}{\gamma_2}$, the expression in [ ] is positive and decreases as t increases. Since the exponent $1/(\varkappa-1)$ is negative, K will decrease. We have

$$K \to \left[-\frac{\gamma_1 b}{\gamma_2}\right]^{\frac{1}{1-\varkappa}}. \qquad (6.\,3.\,6)$$

As one might have expected this limit is the larger the larger is γ_1 and the smaller is $|\gamma_2|$.

If $B < -\frac{\gamma_1 b}{\gamma_2}$, while [ ] is still positive, K will approach the limit (6.3.6) as above, but from the opposite side.

Case 2): $\varkappa < 1$, $\gamma_2 > 0$. When $B > 0$, the expression in [ ] is positive and increases as t increases. Then K will increase beyond limits.

Case 3): $\varkappa > 1$, $\gamma_2 < 0$. If $B > -\frac{\gamma_1 b}{\gamma_2}$, the expression in [ ] is positive and increases as t increases. K will then decrease and approach 0.

If $0 < B < -\frac{\gamma_1 b}{\gamma_2}$, K will increase and will become infinite for a finite value of t.

Case 4): $\varkappa > 1$, $\gamma_2 > 0$. If $B > 0$, the expression in [ ] will reach zero for a finite value of t. Hence K will tend to infinity as t approaches a finite value.

The only case that can lead to a meaningful stability is, therefore, Case 1). It is seen, also, that the initial conditions (the arbitrary constant B) here play an important rôle in determining the form of evolution of the system.

The special cases $\varkappa = 1$ and $\gamma_2 = 0$ may also be mentioned.

If $\varkappa = 1$, we have

$$K = K_o e^{(\gamma_1 b + \gamma_2)t}, \qquad (6.\,3.\,7)$$

where K_0 is an arbitrary constant.

If $\varkappa \neq 1$, $\gamma_2 = 0$, we have

$$K = \frac{1}{[(1-\varkappa)\gamma_1 bt + B_o]^{\frac{1}{\varkappa-1}}}, \qquad (6.\,3.\,8)$$

where B_o is an arbitrary constant.

6. 4. *An Alternative Non-Linear Production Function*

We assume now that the production function has the following form:

$$X = A + \varkappa_1 K + \varkappa_2 K^2, \qquad (6.\,4.\,1)$$

while the process of capital accumulation is given by the equation

$$\dot{K} = \gamma_1 X + \gamma_2 K + \gamma_0. \qquad (6.\,4.\,2)$$

Combining these two equations, we obtain

$$\dot{K} = \gamma_1 \varkappa_2 K^2 + (\gamma_1 \varkappa_1 + \gamma_2)K + \gamma_1 A + \gamma_0. \qquad (6.\,4.\,3)$$

It may be reasonable to assume that A and γ_1 are positive, and that γ_0 is negative, while $\varkappa_1$, $\varkappa_2$, and γ_2 may be either positive or negative (or zero) (except that $\varkappa_1$ and $\varkappa_2$ should not both be negative or zero at the same time). If we write (6. 4. 3) as

$$\dot{K} = A_2 K^2 + A_1 K + A_o \qquad (6.\,4.\,4.a)$$

we have the following possibilities:

$$A_2 = \gamma_1 \varkappa_2 \gtreqless 0, \qquad (6.\,4.\,5)$$

$$A_1 = \gamma_1 \varkappa_1 + \gamma_2 \gtreqless 0, \qquad (6.\,4.\,6)$$

$$A_0 = \gamma_1 A + \gamma_o \gtreqless 0. \qquad (6.\,4.\,7)$$

(6. 4. 4 a) has the following stationary solutions (provided $A_2 \neq 0$):

$$\bar{K} = \frac{-A_1 \pm \sqrt{A_1^2 - 4A_2A_0}}{2A_2}. \tag{6. 4. 8}$$

If these particular solutions should have a concrete meaning in the present case, they must be real and positive. In order that the stationary solutions should be real we must have

$$A_1^2 - 4A_2A_0 \geq 0. \tag{6. 4. 9}$$

Regardless of whether $\bar{K}$ is real or complex, we can write (6. 4. 4. a) as follows:

$$\dot{K} = A_2 ([K - a]^2 - \beta^2), \tag{6. 4. 4.b}$$

where

$$a = -\frac{A_1}{2A_2}, \tag{6. 4. 10}$$

$$\beta = \frac{\sqrt{A_1^2 - 4A_2A_0}}{2|A_2|}. \tag{6. 4. 11}$$

From (6. 4. 4. b) we have, if β^2 is positive,

$$\frac{dK}{[K-a]^2 - \beta^2} = A_2 dt \tag{6. 4. 12}$$

and if β^2 is negative

$$\frac{dK}{[K-a]^2 + (-\beta^2)} = A_2 dt. \tag{6. 4. 13}$$

From (6. 4. 12) we obtain

$$-\frac{1}{\beta} \operatorname{ctnh}^{-1}\left(\frac{K-a}{\beta}\right) = A_2 t + C, \text{ if } (K - a)^2 > \beta^2 \tag{6. 4. 14}$$

and

$$\frac{1}{\beta} \tanh^{-1}\left(\frac{K-a}{\beta}\right) = -A_2 t + C, \text{ if } (K - a)^2 < \beta^2. \tag{6. 4. 15}$$

From (6. 4. 13) we have

$$\frac{1}{\sqrt{-\beta^2}} \tan^{-1}\left(\frac{K-a}{\sqrt{-\beta^2}}\right) = A_2 t + C. \tag{6. 4. 16}$$

Solving the last three equations, we obtain,

$$K = \beta \operatorname{ctnh}(-\beta A_2 t - \beta C) + a, \tag{6. 4. 14.a}$$

34

$$K = \beta \tanh(-\beta A_2 t + \beta C) + \alpha, \qquad (6.\,4.\,15.a)$$

$$K = \sqrt{-\beta^2} \tan(\sqrt{-\beta^2}\,A_2 t + \sqrt{-\beta^2}\,C) + \alpha. \qquad (6.\,4.\,16.a)$$

In these equations C denotes an arbitrary constant of integration. The general form of the solution may also be written as follows,

$$K = \frac{(\alpha-\beta) + B(\alpha+\beta)e^{-2\beta A_2 t}}{1 + Be^{-2\beta A_2 t}}, \qquad (6.\,4.\,17)$$

where B denotes an arbitrary constant.

Whether or not a solution converges towards a stationary level depends in part on the initial conditions of the system, that is, on the value of the arbitrary parameter B.

We have, from (6.4.17),

$$K_o = \frac{(\alpha-\beta) + (\alpha+\beta)B}{1 + B}, \text{ or } B = -\frac{K_o-(\alpha-\beta)}{K_o-(\alpha+\beta)}. \quad (6.\,4.\,18)$$

In order that K should converge to a stationary level it is, in general, necessary that the denominator of (6.4.17) does not change sign as t increases.

The possible stable stationary levels of K are

$$\left.\begin{array}{ll} (\alpha-\beta), & \text{if } \beta A_2 > 0, \\ (\alpha+\beta), & \text{if } \beta A_2 < 0. \end{array}\right\} \qquad (6.\,4.\,19)$$

Whether or not a stationary state is reached depends on K_0. In addition we must here require that the stationary level be non-negative.

If the roots (6.4.8) are complex, there is no possible stationary solution of the system. If a) this is the case, or b) if the possible stable stationary level is negative or c) if B is such that K does not approach a possible stable positive stationary level, then K will in general either go toward infinity or it will reach zero for a finite value of t.

The corresponding time functions for X can be derived by inserting the expressions for K into (6.4.1). If K has a stationary level so does X. The manner in which X will change when K increases depends essentially on the sign of $\varkappa_2$.

The model above illustrates the importance of the initial conditions with regard to the question of stability, when the system is non-linear.

35

7. MODELS FOR A STATIONARY POPULATION, CONTINUED. GROWTH OF CAPITAL AND OF KNOW-HOW REGARDED AS SEPARATE VARIABLES

In the preceding models one could think of the accumulated capital K as a combined index including the accumulation of material means of production as well as of knowledge and technical know-how. We shall now consider some models where the level of know-how, S, is brought in explicitly as a variable.

7. 1. *Trends due to the Accumulation of Knowledge*

Let the production function be linear in K and S, e.g.

$$X = A + \varkappa K + \sigma S, \qquad (7.1.1)$$

while the growth of capital is given by the linear relation

$$\dot{K} = \gamma_1 X + \gamma_2 K + \gamma_3 S + \gamma_0. \qquad (7.1.2)$$

Here X is the level of production, K the accumulated amount of physical capital and S some index of the level of education and technical know-how.

We shall assume that S is a linear function of time. The meaning of this assumption is that S is a linear function of the 'length of experience' of the society considered. We write

$$S = \mu t + \mu_0, \qquad (7.1.3)$$

where μ and μ_0 are constants.

From this system we obtain

$$\dot{K} = (\gamma_1 \varkappa + \gamma_2) K + \mu (\gamma_1 \sigma + \gamma_3) t + (\gamma_1 A + \gamma_1 \sigma \mu_0 + \\ + \gamma_3 \mu_0 + \gamma_0) \qquad (7.1.4)$$

The general solution of (7. 1. 4) is

$$K = B e^{(\gamma_1 \varkappa + \gamma_2)t} + A_1 t + A_0 \qquad (7.1.5)$$

where B is arbitrary, while A_1 and A_0 are constants depending on the parameters of the system. We have

$$A_1 = \frac{-\mu(\gamma_1 \sigma + \gamma_3)}{\gamma_1 \varkappa + \gamma_2}, \qquad (7.1.6)$$

$$A_o = - \frac{\mu(\gamma_1\sigma + \gamma_3) + (\gamma_1 A + \gamma_1\sigma\mu_o + \gamma_3\mu_o + \gamma_o)(\gamma_1\varkappa + \gamma_2)}{(\gamma_1\varkappa + \gamma_2)^2}. \qquad (7.1.7)$$

If K_o is the value of K at $t = 0$, we have

$$B = K_o - A_o. \qquad (7.1.8)$$

If $(\gamma_1\varkappa + \gamma_2) > 0$ and $B > 0$, K will increase beyond limits, regardless of the values of A_1 and A_o. But the speed of development will depend on the nature of the trend (7.1.3). Given the value of K_o, the coefficient B also depends on the coefficients of the trend for S. (Cfr. (7.1.7) and (7.1.8)).

If $(\gamma_1\varkappa + \gamma_2) < 0$, the first member to the right in (7.1.5) will tend to zero. Then the denominator in (7.1.6) will be negative. If then $\mu(\gamma_1\sigma + \gamma_3) > 0$, A_1 will be positive, i.e. K will have an increasing trend. This could perhaps be interpreted in the following way: A negative γ_2 means that an increase in K leads to a feeling of 'saturation' that tends to reduce further capital accumulation. But a positive γ_3, i.e. 'a growing understanding of the importance of accumulation', may to some extent counteract the saturation effect. If, on the other hand, γ_3 is negative and sufficiently large in absolute value, A_1 may be negative. K will then eventually reach a zero level.

The corresponding results for X are obvious.

7.2. Influence of Capital Accumulation upon the Growth of Education and Know-How

Let the production function and the law of capital accumulation be the same as in the preceding section, i.e.

$$X = A + \varkappa K + \sigma S \qquad (7.2.1)$$

$$\dot{K} = \gamma_1 X + \gamma_2 K + \gamma_3 S + \gamma_0, \qquad (7.2.2)$$

but assume now that the growth of the index of education, S, is given by

$$\dot{S} = \mu_o \int_0^t e^{\mu(t-\tau)} \dot{K}(\tau) d\tau \qquad (7.2.3)$$

where μ_o and μ are constants, $\mu_o > 0$, $\mu < 0$. This assumption

37

means that the 'educational effect' at point of time t of a dose of capital invested at $\tau < t$ tapers off exponentially as $(t-\tau)$ increases.

From the system above we have

$$\dot{K} = (\gamma_1\varkappa + \gamma_2)K + (\gamma_1\sigma + \gamma_3)S + (\gamma_1 A + \gamma_0). \qquad (7.\,2.\,4)$$

Differentiating (7. 2. 4) with respect to t, we get

$$\ddot{K} = (\gamma_1\varkappa + \gamma_2)\,\dot{K} + (\gamma_1\sigma + \gamma_3)\mu_0\!\!\int\limits_0^t e^{\mu(t-\tau)}\,\dot{K}(\tau)d\tau. \qquad (7.\,2.\,5)$$

The general solution of (7. 2. 5) is

$$K = B_1 e^{\varrho_1 t} + B_2 e^{\varrho_2 t} + B_o, \qquad (7.\,2.\,6)$$

where B_o and B_1 or B_2 (but not both) are arbitrary constants which may be determined by initial conditions. ϱ_1 and ϱ_2 are the two roots of the characteristic equation

$$\varrho^2 - (\mu + \gamma_1\varkappa + \gamma_2)\varrho + ((\gamma_1\varkappa + \gamma_2)\mu - (\gamma_1\sigma + \gamma_3)\mu_0) = 0. \qquad (7.\,2.\,7)$$

B_1 and B_2 are related by the condition

$$B_1\frac{\varrho_1}{\varrho_1 - \mu} + B_2\frac{\varrho_2}{\varrho_2 - \mu} = 0. \qquad (7.\,2.\,8)$$

The roots ϱ_1 and ϱ_2 may be real or complex, and the solution (7. 2. 6) may be damped, undamped or explosive, depending on the signs and the values of the structural coefficients.

If the solution is damped, the stationary level that is approached is *arbitrary*, unless additional initial conditions are imposed.

Under realistic assumptions concerning the structural coefficients the roots of (7. 2. 7) will be real. This is seen as follows:

The condition that the roots be real is that

$$(\mu + (\gamma_1\varkappa + \gamma_2))^2 - 4\,((\gamma_1\varkappa + \gamma_2)\mu - (\gamma_1\sigma + \gamma_3)\mu_0) \geq 0 \qquad (7.\,2.\,9)$$

But the left hand side of (7. 2. 9) is equal to

$$(\mu - (\gamma_1\varkappa + \gamma_2))^2 + 4\,(\gamma_1\sigma + \gamma_3)\mu_0.$$

Thus, if γ_1, σ, γ_3, and μ_0 are all positive, which is reasonable, (7. 2. 9) is fulfilled.

S and X may now easily be calculated from (7. 2. 3) and (7. 2. 1), using (7. 2. 6). S will grow as long as K is increasing, and would continue to grow for some time even if K should subsequently start decreasing; (the 'after-effect' of a period of expansion). X could also continue to grow after a period of an expanding K has ended because of a continued growth in S. (These conclusions are generally inconsistent with an assumption of a stationary level of K.)

8. POPULATION GROWTH AND THE ACCUMULATION PROCESS

The relations that connect population growth and capital accumulation may take on a variety of forms but the basic considerations behind them would seem to be the following: 1) The growth of population is, in part, determined by the economic level of subsistence that the region can provide. 2) The volume of production is determined by the available man-power and the amount of capital and know-how. 3) The rate of capital accumulation is the result of a balance between the desire to consume and the desire to provide for the future. And 4) the nature of this network of relations must be assumed to depend on the educational level of the economic region considered, this educational level being itself — at least in part — a result of the process of past economic development.

We shall consider a few simple models that incorporate some or all of these ideas.

8. 1. *The Generalized 'Logistic' in a System with Capital Accumulation*

We shall consider a simple model corresponding to the one in section 5. 1, viz.

$$\frac{\dot{N}}{N} = a - \beta \frac{N}{X} \qquad (8. 1. 1.)$$

$$X = a_1 N + a_2 K \qquad (8. 1. 2)$$

$$\dot{K} = \gamma_1 X + \gamma_2 N + \gamma_3 K. \qquad (8. 1. 3)$$

Here $N =$ total population (variation in the age distribution neglected, as in the previous models), $X =$ total production, and

39

K = the amount of capital. We shall assume here, to simplify the mathematics, that it be possible to define the amount of capital, K, (including 'original' resources) in such a way that it is permissible not to add any constant terms to the right hand sides of (8. 1. 2) and (8. 1. 3). This is, admittedly, a strong restriction but the system may, nevertheless, serve to illustrate certain basic features of the interrelation between population growth and capital formation.

The system (8. 1. 1)–(8. 1. 3) does not in general have a stationary solution except the trivial solution $X = K = N = 0$. It has, however, a 'quasi-equilibrium' solution $\frac{X}{N}$ = constant and $\frac{K}{N}$ = constant. This is seen as follows.

Assuming $\frac{K}{N} = \bar{k}$ = constant and $\frac{X}{N} = \bar{x} = a_1 + a_2\bar{k}$ = constant (because of (8. 1. 2)), the system (8. 1. 1)–(8. 1. 3) becomes

$$\frac{\dot{N}}{N} = a - \frac{\beta}{a_1 + a_2\bar{k}}, \qquad (8.\ 1.\ 1a)$$

$$\frac{\dot{K}}{K} = (\gamma_1 a_2 + \gamma_3)\bar{k} + (\gamma_1 a_1 + \gamma_2). \qquad (8.\ 1.\ 3a)$$

If $\frac{K}{N}$ is to be identically equal to a constant $\bar{k}$, we have from (8. 1. 1. a)

$$N = N_0 e^{\varrho t}, \ \varrho = a - \frac{\beta}{a_1 + a_2\bar{k}}, \qquad (8.\ 1.\ 1.b)$$

and from (8. 1. 3. a),

$$K = \frac{[(\gamma_1 a_2 + \gamma_3)\bar{k} + (\gamma_1 a_1 + \gamma_2)]N_0}{\varrho} e^{\varrho t} + B, \qquad (8.\ 1.\ 3.b)$$

where B is a constant of integration.

These solutions for N and K satisfy $\frac{K}{N}$ = constant *if* $B = 0$. The question is now whether there exists a constant $\bar{k}$ such that

$$\bar{k} = \frac{[(\gamma_1 a_2 + \gamma_3)\bar{k} + (\gamma_1 a_1 + \gamma_2)](a_1 + a_2\bar{k})}{aa_1 - \beta + aa_2\bar{k}}. \qquad (8.\ 1.\ 4)$$

This is an equation of 2nd degree in $\bar{k}$. It has in general two roots $\bar{k} = \bar{k}_1$, and $\bar{k} = \bar{k}_2$.

If the roots $\bar{k}_1$ and $\bar{k}_2$ are real there are, therefore, two possibilities of $\dfrac{K}{N}\left(\text{and therefore also } \dfrac{X}{N}\right)$ remaining constant while X, K, and N develop exponentially. But only one of the roots represents a stable solution of this nature. If this root is negative, the system has no meaningfull 'quasi-equilibrium'.

If the roots $\bar{k}_1$ and $\bar{k}_2$ are complex, the system has no 'quasi-equilibrium' solution.

If a positive, stable 'quasi-equilibrium' exists, the question of whether or nor it is reached depends on the initial conditions of the system, in much the same manner as was found for the system discussed in section 6. 4.

The 'quasi-equilibrium', if it exists, depends in a somewhat complicated way, upon all the structural coefficients of the system (8. 1. 1)–(8. 1. 3).

From the system (8. 1. 1)–(8. 1. 3) we derive

$$\frac{K}{N}\frac{\dot{N}}{N} = a\frac{K}{N} - \beta\frac{\dfrac{K}{N}}{a_1 + a_2\dfrac{K}{N}} \tag{8. 1. 5}$$

$$\frac{\dot{K}}{N} = (\gamma_1 a_1 + \gamma_2) + (\gamma_1 a_2 + \gamma_3)\frac{K}{N} \tag{8. 1. 6}$$

Subtracting (8. 1. 5) from (8. 1. 6) and using the notation $k = \dfrac{K}{N}$, we obtain

$$\dot{k} = \frac{(\gamma_1 a_2 + \gamma_3 - a)a_2 k^2 + [(\gamma_1 a_2 + \gamma_3)a_1 + (\gamma_1 a_1 + \gamma_2)a_2 - aa_1 + \beta]k + (\gamma_1 a_1 + \gamma_2)a_1}{a_1 + a_2 k}. \tag{8. 1. 7}$$

Or, introducing shorter notations for the coefficients,

$$\dot{k} = A\frac{k^2 + A_1 k + A_0}{k + A_2}. \tag{8. 1. 8}$$

The general solution of (8. 1. 8) has one of the following forms:

$$\text{Log}\,|k^2 + A_1 k + A_0| - \frac{4A_2 - 2A_1}{\sqrt{A_1^2 - 4A_0}}\,\text{ctnh}^{-1}\!\left(\frac{2k + A_1}{\sqrt{A_1^2 - 4A_0}}\right) = 2A(t + C), \tag{8. 1. 9.a}$$

$$\text{Log}\,|k^2 + A_1 k + A_0| - \frac{4A_2 - 2A_1}{\sqrt{A_1^2 - 4A_0}}\,\text{tanh}^{-1}\!\left(\frac{2k + A_1}{\sqrt{A_1^2 - 4A_0}}\right) = 2A(t + C), \tag{8. 1. 9.b}$$

41

$$\text{Log}(k^2 + A_1 k + A_0) + \frac{4A_2 - 2A_1}{\sqrt{4A_0 - A_1^2}} \tan^{-1}\left(\frac{2k + A_1}{\sqrt{4A_0 - A_1^2}}\right) = 2A(t + C),$$

$$(8.\,1.\,9.c)$$

where C denotes an arbitrary constant of integration.

The asymptotic properties of these solutions have already been discussed.

8.2. *An Alternative Generalization of the 'Logistic' in a System with Capital Accumulation*

Let us consider a system which is essentially the same as that in 8.1, except that we now assume that the growth of population depends directly on the available amount of capital. More specifically, we may assume that the death rate of the population varies inversely with the level of capital per head. (Accumulated stocks prevent acute starvation. Better housing, easier work, more hospitals etc. lengthen expectation of life, and so on).

The simple system considered is the following:

$$\frac{\dot{N}}{N} = a - \beta \frac{N}{K}, \qquad (8.\,2.\,1)$$

$$X = a_1 N + a_2 K, \qquad (8.\,2.\,2)$$

$$\dot{K} = \gamma_1 X + \gamma_2 N + \gamma_3 K. \qquad (8.\,2.\,3)$$

(We have omitted constant terms, as in the previous model.)

From these equations we derive

$$\frac{K}{N}\frac{\dot{N}}{N} = a\frac{K}{N} - \beta, \qquad (8.\,2.\,1.a)$$

$$\frac{\dot{K}}{N} = (\gamma_1 a_1 + \gamma_2) + (\gamma_1 a_2 + \gamma_3)\frac{K}{N}. \qquad (8.\,2.\,4)$$

Subtracting (8.2.1.a) from (8.2.4) and introducing the notation $\frac{K}{N} = k$, we have

$$\dot{k} = (\gamma_1 a_2 + \gamma_3 - a)k + (\gamma_1 a_1 + \gamma_2 + \beta) \qquad (8.\,2.\,5)$$

The solution of (8.2.5) is

$$k = \left(k_0 + \frac{\gamma_1 a_1 + \gamma_2 + \beta}{\gamma_1 a_2 + \gamma_3 - a}\right) e^{(\gamma_1 a_2 + \gamma_3 - a)t} - \frac{\gamma_1 a_1 + \gamma_2 + \beta}{\gamma_1 a_2 + \gamma_3 - a} \qquad (8.\,2.\,6)$$

where k_0 is the initial value of k at $t = 0$.

If $\gamma_1 a_2 + \gamma_3 - a < 0$, k will converge towards a stationary level. This may be the case if a is large or if γ_3 has a large negative value. If the stationary level is positive, it will then be the larger the larger is β and the smaller the smaller is a.

When $(\gamma_1 a_2 + \gamma_3 - a) > 0$, k will expand (if k_o is sufficiently large) and this expansion will be the more rapid the smaller is a and the larger is γ_3.

If k is increasing, population will grow at an increasing rate (or decrease at a retarding rate). If k approaches a constant level, *the rate of increase* of population will approach a constant.

8. 3. *Influence upon Birth Rate of the Level of Education*

This influence is certainly a very complicated one. Here we shall consider the extremely simple (but perhaps not entirely unrealistic) case when the birth rate varies inversely with some index of the 'level of education', S. We consider the following system:

$$\frac{\dot{N}}{N} = \frac{a}{1 + \sigma S} - \beta \frac{N}{K}, \qquad (8.\,3.\,1)$$

$$X = a_1 N + a_2 K, \qquad (8.\,3.\,2)$$

$$\dot{K} = \gamma_1 X + \gamma_2 N + \gamma_3 K. \qquad (8.\,3.\,3)$$

As before, N means population, X production, and K the amount of capital. We further make a very simple assumption about the index of education, S, viz. that it varies directly with the amount of accumulated capital per head,

$$S = \mu \frac{K}{N} + \mu_o. \qquad (8.\,3.\,4)$$

This system leads to the following equation for the amount of capital *per head*

$$\dot{k} = \frac{(\gamma_1 a_2 + \gamma_3)\,\sigma\mu k^2 + [(\gamma_1 a_2 + \gamma_3)\,(1 + \sigma\mu_o) + (\gamma_1 a_1 + \gamma_2 + \beta)\,\sigma\mu - a]k + (\gamma_1 a_1 + \gamma_2 + \beta)\,(1 + \sigma\mu_o)}{\sigma\mu k + \sigma\mu_o + 1}.$$
$$(8.\,3.\,5)$$

This is an equation similar to (8. 1. 6). The discussion of its

43

solution, the possible 'quasi-equilibria', etc., can be carried out in the same way as in 8. 1, and will not be repeated here.

The models that we have discussed in the preceding four sections are, of course, only examples out of an endless variety of possibilities for specifying such models. But those that have been discussed are perhaps sufficient to illustrate certain general properties of such models that are of particular interest in a study of interregional dissimilarities. These general properties will be examined further in the following Part III.

III. DETERMINISTIC THEORIES
OF EVOLUTIONARY DISSIMILARITIES

From the analysis in the preceding sections it is evident that, even if we consider only very simple models, they can give rise to a great variety of different time-paths. This is true even if we consider only the effects of changing the values of the parameters in a particular model. One could then ask why we should think it strange that various economic regions actually have developed very differently. Would it not have been as strange if they had all been alike?

If it were possible to trace the differences in development back to certain natural and unavoidable dissimilarities, there would not seem to be much reason for further curiosity. But even our simple models indicate that human behavior also plays a rôle, sometimes even a decisive one, in shaping the paths of progress. And the simple answer that people are different is not very satisfying. In fact, if we have any belief in the fundamentals of economic theory, we *cannot* accept such an answer without asking *why* people act differently.

If we take some simple model of economic growth as a starting point, we shall, therefore, want to make further studies of the formal conditions for dissimilar developments, how such conditions could in fact arise, and why they could persist over a long, perhaps indefinite, period of time.

9. CLASSIFICATION OF POSSIBLE DISSIMILARITIES

One could think of the various models that we have discussed in the preceding sections as describing developments in different regions. However, we want to assume now that the theoretical objective is not to search for a particular model for each region, but to look for a *general model* where regional differences can be covered simply by changing the values of certain parameters.

Most of the models so far considered could be thought of as special cases of the following general dynamic system:

$$X = \varphi(N, K, S, t; a_1, a_2, \ldots, a_h),$$ (9.1)

$$\dot{N} = \psi(N, K, X, S, t; \beta_1, \beta_2, \ldots, \beta_k),$$ (9.2.)

$$\dot{K} = f(N, K, X, S, t; \gamma_1, \gamma_2, \ldots, \gamma_m),$$ (9.3)

$$\dot{S} = g(N, K, X, S, t; \delta_1, \delta_2, \ldots, \delta_n).$$ (9.4)

Here X, N, K, S mean 'production', 'population', 'capital', and 'education', respectively. The a's, β's, γ's and δ's are structural parameters of the system.

We could consider this system as a special form of an even more general system in terms of functional equations, viz.

$$\Phi\left[\overset{t}{\underset{t_0}{N(\tau)}}, \overset{t}{\underset{t_0}{K(\tau)}}, \overset{t}{\underset{t_0}{X(\tau)}}, \overset{t}{\underset{t_0}{S(\tau)}}; t, a_1, a_2, \ldots, a_h\right] = 0,$$ (9.5)

$$\Psi\left[\overset{t}{\underset{t_0}{N(\tau)}}, \overset{t}{\underset{t_0}{K(\tau)}}, \overset{t}{\underset{t_0}{X(\tau)}}, \overset{t}{\underset{t_0}{S(\tau)}}; t, \beta_1, \beta_2, \ldots, \beta_k\right] = 0,$$ (9.6)

$$F\left[\overset{t}{\underset{t_0}{N(\tau)}}, \overset{t}{\underset{t_0}{K(\tau)}}, \overset{t}{\underset{t_0}{X(\tau)}}, \overset{t}{\underset{t_0}{S(\tau)}}; t, \gamma_1, \gamma_2, \ldots, \gamma_m\right] = 0,$$ (9.7)

$$G\left[\overset{t}{\underset{t_0}{N(\tau)}}, \overset{t}{\underset{t_0}{K(\tau)}}, \overset{t}{\underset{t_0}{X(\tau)}}, \overset{t}{\underset{t_0}{S(\tau)}}; t, \delta_1, \delta_2, \ldots, \delta_n\right] = 0,$$ (9.8)

where Φ, Ψ, F, and G are functionals, and where t_0 is the 'starting point' of the economy considered.

Under proper mathematical restrictions such a dynamic system will define a family of time functions, generated by the parameters a, β, γ, and δ, and the value of certain 'initial conditions', e.g. $N(t_0)$, $K(t_0)$, $S(t_0)$, and $X(t_0)$.

If we have been successful in finding a really general and fundamental dynamic model, the functional forms Φ, Ψ, F, and G should be the same for all regions considered. Supposing this to be the case, what are the possibilities of differences in development as between the various regions? If the solution of the system is unique for every admissible set of values of the structural parameters and the initial conditions, interregional differences could occur only as a result of differences in structural parameters and/or the initial conditions.

46

The study of particular models in the preceding sections has shown that changes in the structural coefficients may mean the difference between progress and stagnation, between rapid progress and slow progress, between high values and low values of the variables at a given point of time. We have also seen that, even if two systems (two regions) have the same values of the structural parameters, differences in the initial conditions could mean that one of the regions would expand progressively while the other would move towards stagnation, or that one region would progress much faster than the other. What we have to investigate is whether such formal possibilities of dissimilarities actually could represent meaningful economic hypotheses.

10. THE HYPOTHESIS OF STRUCTURAL DIFFERENCES

The structural coefficients of the system (9. 1)–(9. 4), or (9. 5)–(9. 8), could be grouped into the following four categories:

(A) Parameters describing the 'size' of the region, the disposable natural resources, climatic conditions, etc.

(B) Technological parameters that describe the input – output relations under which the region has to operate.

(C) Parameters related to the presence, the activities, and the decisions of *other* regions, but relevant to the economic activities of the region concerned. (For the time being we shall, somewhat artificially, consider these parameters as given constants).

(D) Parameters characterizing intra-regional behavior, such as the desire and willingness to work, to consume, to procreate, etc.

The problem of grouping the parameters in this way is not as simple as it may appear. Thus, if we have formulated the structural equations by using (in a sense) as few parameters as possible, these parameters must frequently be regarded as *functions of other, more basic, parameters*. For example, if a_1 and a_2 are two such more basic parameters and if they enter into the structural equations only in the form $(a_1 + a_2)$, this expression could be replaced by one single parameter, e.g. β. Here a_1 may be a 'genuinely technical' parameter, a_2 a parameter exclusively related to behavior. But β

47

cannot be classified in any one of the groups. If we want to use a classification as suggested, we have to assume that there exists a finite set of basic and 'unmixed' parameters and that we have either used these parameters explicitly in formulating the structural equations, or that we have used parameters that are known functions of those in the basic set. In simple economic models, such as those frequently found in economic literature, it is often very difficult to discover exactly what is the meaning of the parameters introduced. Each of them usually covers a whole complex of parameters from an earlier step in a deductive process. In the following discussion we shall assume that the parameters in (9. 1)–(9. 4) actually are of such a basic nature that the classification suggested makes sense when applied directly to the a's, the β's etc. However, there are many philosophical questions that could be raised in this connection. Some of them will be considered later in this section.

We shall now study the meaning of interregional differences in the structural parameters a little more closely.

Among the parameters in category (A) the most obvious ones are those that measure the geographic area of a region, the arable land, ore deposits, etc. But measurement may be difficult because of qualitative differences. Also, it is a question whether any index of the 'amount of resources' could have a definite meaning except in relation to the particular technique of utilization that is being applied at any given time.

However, in order to stay within an analytically manageable framework we have to pay the price of simplification. From the point of view of a macro-dynamic theory it then seems plausible to introduce the theoretical notion of the 'economic size' of a region and to assume that this concept can be described by certain parameters. These parameters could be thought of as natural constraint upon the scale of economic activity in a given region.

It may be that part of the interregional differences in these natural scale factors can be eliminated simply by some sort of 'deflation', e.g. by using figures 'per capita', 'per square mile', etc. In the models of economic growth discussed in Part II we have to a large extent relied on such possibilities of simplification. However, the underlying assumption is then some sort of constant return to scale which undoubtedly at best covers only part of the truth.

Certain genuine and basic differences in natural conditions would no doubt remain whatever be the indices of 'deflation' that we invent to make the various regions comparable in this respect. However, it is far from obvious that such differences need play any decisive rôle in a regional network with wide opportunities for trade and intercommunication. (We shall revert to this point in Part V.)

The notion of *technological* parameters is somewhat more complicated than it may at first appear. Economists usually like to think that description and measurement of such parameters may simply be imported from the field of engineering. To some extent this also holds true. The output of certain types of products may be almost uniquely determined by the nature of the raw materials and the machinery used. It may even be possible to describe inputs of certain types of labor in such technical detail that we are able to say a priori with great precision what will be the result of applying a certain quantity of labor upon particular resources. In other words, we know — and much of this knowledge is of very old date — a good deal about particular technological input – output relations. But it is a hopeless task to describe all productive activities in a whole region in purely technological terms. No matter what actual productive processes we think of, we almost always find that they contain some organizational element. This means that even if we go very far in an attempted technological subdivision of the processes of production, the human elements involved could still give room for alternative results, or 'different ways of doing the same thing'. And the more we want to think in terms of aggregates, the farther we move away from a purely technological notion of the economic processes of transformation. This means that very often the parameters that we call technological, actually are more related to human choice and human behavior than to chemical formulae and laws of mechanics.

But there is another aspect of the notion of technological coefficients which is perhaps even more important from our point of view here, viz. the question to what extent the coefficients can be assumed to be *known* to the people concerned. Obviously the degree of knowledge in this respect must have an important, perhaps decisive, influence upon what people actually chose to do at any given time. Let us examine this a little closer.

Suppose that it were in fact possible to single out all kinds of input – output relations as something purely technological that would be *data*, regardless of whether or not human action would bring them into play. We should then have the concept of a very general set of technical transformation functions. It would have to cover all alternatives with regard to natural resources and human or man-made inputs, and also all feasible successions in time of the processes and operations involved. In other words, it would have to cover all conceivable *plans* of production. To assume that the people of a region ever have possessed — or ever will possess — technological omniscience to such an extent is, of course, ridiculous. One must assume that the choice of transformation processes is restricted to a sub-set of alternatives actually known at the time considered. This sub-set of admissible alternatives is then no longer an invariant technological concept but a function of human education and knowledge.

One could try to save the purely technological view by including in the general transformation function some factors describing the degree of human knowledge but, if one carries this view to the bitter end, it does not go very well together with the idea that inputs of human activities are subject to autonomous choice. Thus, for example, the choice of trying to learn new things cannot very easily be thought of as being based on the knowledge of a specific input – output relation of learning.

What are the conclusions to be drawn regarding possible inter-regional dissimilarities due to differences in technological parameters? If we could assume that the knowledge of a general set of possible technological transformations were common to all regions, there could be no other hindrances to the regions being similar than differences in natural resources. If two regions had similar natural resources, their economic differences would have to be ascribed to some present or past differences in human nature in the two regions, in their attitudes and their economic modes of action.

Now, it is easy to point to geographic areas that are not strikingly different in resources necessary for modern industrialization, but which, nevertheless, show enormous differences in the material welfare extracted from those resources. Such dissimilarities would then have to be the result of differences in human nature and conduct.

Regarding the parameters that describe *human attitude and action,* we have made a distinction between those (category (C)) that are external to the region concerned and those (category (D)) that are internal. It is obviously rather drastic to assume that the alternatives of foreign relations open to a given region could be described by means of a few simple parameters. We shall have occasion to study this problem more closely in Part V. For our present purpose the simple assumption is, however, not quite hopeless, for the following reason: Looking at the economic geography of the world today we have no difficulty in finding large areas where 1) economic developments, by present standards, are strikingly different, where at the same time 2) natural conditions are not sufficiently different to make widely diverging paths of development a necessity, and where 3) the technological opportunities of rapid progress would not seem to depend in any essential way upon foreign trade.

What could cause a large divergence in development between such otherwise similar regions? It may be that the phenomenon cannot be explained except by assuming that, *somehow,* one or more of the regions got a head start and that the divergence grew by its own momentum, by suppressing and exploiting other regions, etc. But such a hypotheses would take us beyond the one we are studying in this section, viz. the hypothesis of dissimilarities due to differences in structural coefficients. In any case, it certainly does not look any easier, a priori, to explain disparities between regions that are in contact with each other than to explain disparities between isolated regions. But we have yet to discuss what divergencies could be caused by the human element in two otherwise similar regions. For this purpose we may as well assume that the regions concerned are isolated.

In the various models in Part II it was shown that behavioristic parameters describing the desire to work, to save, to procreate, to learn etc. may play a decisive rôle in shaping the path of eco-

51

nomic development of a given region. Hence, if one is satisfied by the explanation that 'people are different' in these respects, there would be no need for further speculations upon the reason for dissimilarities. And, of course, such an explanation does not need to have anything to do with the question of general and equal respect for all peoples, whatever their ways of life may be. However, there are undoubtedly many among us who do not want to terminate the — admittedly endless — process of asking 'why' at this stage. That is, we may prefer to maintain the idea that people are essentially alike unless we could find objective reasons why they are not.

Now, if the statement that people are alike means that the behavioristic parameters in a rigid dynamic model are the same for all regions, we have no other possibilities of dissimilarities, due to structural differences, than those already discussed. But could it not be that the general assumption of people being alike covers something which is not the same thing as equal behavioristic parameters in a dynamic economic model? In this connection the idea of differences due to different 'environments' is very near at hand. The question then is what we mean by environment. Within the framework of a rigid dynamic model of the type considered above, the meaning of environment can be expressed as follows: The economic environment of a regional population at time t is the history of the variables X, N, K, S up to and including the point of time t, together with the parameters that are given by nature (the resources etc.). But from such a notion of environment we shall not easily escape the conclusion that in all 'old' regions the environments are themselves to a large extent man-made. Thus, we are back with the same question again, viz. why people, if they are by nature alike, may have chosen to act in apparently very different ways. The only tangible reason that we have been able to produce as yet is that the naturally given environments were different from the start.

Our analysis of the exact-model approach has thus far left us with no particularly satisfactory answer to the problem of explaining dissimilarities. But we have still to investigate the rôle that differences in initial conditions could play. However, before we come to that, there is another aspect of our problem, which we have already touched, but which deserves closer attention: The relation between the *degree* of dissimilarity in structural coefficients and the corresponding *degree* of dissimilarity in long-range developments. Thus, if it be possible that even small differences in the structural coefficients could, in the long run, lead to very large disparities in the variables that we have chosen as indicators of economic development, we might be less concerned about the intricate philosophical questions discussed in the foregoing.

From the simple models considered in Part II it is evident that even very small differences in structural coefficients (e.g. small percentage differences) can produce very large discrepancies in development, provided that sufficient time is allowed to elapse before a comparison is made. As an example, consider those models where the time-path of the accumulated capital, K, is given by an exponential function $K = Ae^{\varrho t} + B$. (Cf. e.g. the models in 6. 1 and 6. 2). Suppose that there are two regions, No. 1 and No. 2, whose capital developments are given by $K_1 = A_1 e^{\varrho_1 t} + B_1$, and $K_2 = A_2 e^{\varrho_2 t} + B_2$, respectively, where A_1, A_2, B_1, B_2 are positive constants. Assume that ϱ_1 and ϱ_2 are positive constants such that, due e.g. to a slight difference in the 'propensity to save' in the two regions, $\varrho_1 + \varepsilon = \varrho_2$ when ε is an arbitrary small but fixed positive quantity. It is then seen that the difference $K_2(t) - K_1(t)$ will grow with increasing speed. In fact, even the *ratio* K_2/K_1 increases beyond limits as t goes to infinity. Similar statements may hold for other models where the solutions are more complicated.

On the other hand, we have models among those considered, where the statements above would not hold, at least not for each parameter of behavior taken separately. (Cf. e.g. the model in 6. 3.) If a model is such that it has stable solutions approaching a finite level, this level may be rather inelastic with regard to changes in some of the behavioristic parameters. In other cases, however, the stationary level may be very sensitive to changes in the values of the behavioristic parameters. (Cf. e.g. the solution for k in the model 8. 2.)

With regard to the mathematical reasoning above one could object that, after all, the values of the variables, at time t, in a dynamic system are mere transformations of the structural parameters. Therefore, if one decides to call certain differences in the values of the variables 'large', why then describe the corresponding differences between the parameters as 'small'? One could say that a distinction between large and small is here highly arbitrary, merely a question of transformation of units. However, from the point of view of *economics* the distinction may make more sense. We might look upon the matter this way:

Consider the parameters of behavior as something that could conceivably be altered by human decision. A change in the parameters would in general mean some immediate change in the economic life of the region, maybe less consumption, higher rate of accumulation, lower birth rate, etc. Now, if we consider two regions starting with the same initial conditions, but with a slight difference in the parameters of behavior, the economic ways of life in the two regions may for a considerable time remain almost alike, by all practical standards. E.g. by a slightly higher rate of accumulation one of the regions may not have to sacrifice much in the way of current standard of living as compared with the other region. If one particular set of values of the behavior parameters are in a sense optimal to the tastes and attitudes of the population, a slight deviation from this optimum may not really mean a noticable sacrifice. But in the long run this slight sacrifice may cumulate into a very big future gain.

It seems that here we have touched upon a real possibility of explaining dissimilarities in long-range developments, even on the basis of simple and rigid dynamic models. But the question is of course whether a model that actually reproduces historic patterns of economic developments and, at the same time makes sense from the point of view of economic theory, could be made to fit the data for each region without admitting large differences in the parameters involved. This is, in the end, an econometric problem. However, there is reason for scepticism towards this type of 'explanation'. The speed with which the Western industrialized regions have developed during the last hundred years as against relative slow progress or stagnation in many of the backward areas, would seem to imply more substantial structural differences.

11. THE HYPOTHESIS OF 'LAGS' AND 'LEADS'

A methodological principle of some standing among historians is that of cross-section studies: By looking at the ways of life found among savage and backward people today one can — it is held — learn much about how the ancient forefathers of 'modern' countries lived. This belief is strengthened by the fact that archaeologic research in modern countries has uncovered tools and implements resembling those still in use among certain under-developed peoples.

The argument certainly carries a good deal of conviction, but it also leaves some rather fundamental questions unanswered. Suppose we take the point of view that the people in backward areas have *stagnated* at a level that people in advanced areas had many centuries ago. Unless we think of this phenomenon as a mere accident, we have a problem of explaining how various regions could develop so differently. We might very well think that they have been different 'to begin with'. But then the principle of analogy between the cross-section picture and the evolutionary picture becomes somewhat problematic. Suppose, on the other hand, we think that the cross-section dissimilarities are due to the fact that certain areas 'have *not yet* developed', they are 'behind', implying that the difference is only a question of time. Why is it then that many of the areas, historically described as the 'oldest', are among those that today are called backward?

It is not always clear which of these two views is behind the methodological principle mentioned. From the terminology used in history books one gets the feeling that every country or region is in some sort of evolutionary process. Popular opinion certainly tends to lean strongly to the view that cross-section dissimilarities are just a matter of time, that evolution in the various regions moves with 'lags', or 'leads'.

We want to investigate these ideas further in light of determinate dynamic models of the type (9. 5)–(9. 8). On the basis of such a theoretical framework a precise description of the hypothesis of 'lags' and 'leads' could be formulated as follows: Suppose we have two regions the economic evolution of which could be described by a dynamic system of the form (9. 5)–(9. 8) (by appropriate choice of parameters to fit each region). Assume that, under given initial conditions, the two systems define uniquely the time-paths of the variables for each of the two regions. Consider one of these variables, e.g. the amounts of capital $K_1(t)$ and $K_2(t)$, in the first and second region, respectively. Let $\theta(t)$ be a single-valued function that is non-negative and finite for every value of $t \geq t_o$. If there exists a function $\theta(t)$, having this property, and such that

$$K_1(t) \equiv K_2(t + \theta(t)), \tag{11.1}$$

for every value of $t \geq t_o$, we could say that capital development in the first region 'leads' that in the second region by the finite time interval $\theta(t)$. Conversely we could say that, for $t \geq t_o + \theta(t_o)$, the capital development in the second region 'lags' behind that in the first region by the finite interval $\theta(t)$. The notion of lag or lead could be restricted to a certain finite time interval, $t_1 \geq t \geq t_o$. It might be that for $t \geq t_1$ the rôles of K_1 and K_2 would be reversed, or that the subsequent developments would not fall under the definition of lag or lead as given here.

If we consider a system of the type (9. 5)–(9. 8), different sets of solutions that by comparison exhibit lags or leads as defined above could be produced by varying the structural parameters as well as by varying the values of the initial conditions. Solutions that satisfy the definition of lags or leads may, of course, be very different in many other respects. The practical notion of lags or leads should probably be restricted to cases when $\theta(t)$ is a function with a relatively small maximal value. But then the hypothesis of lags or leads probably could not give a satisfactory explanation of the very big dissimilarities that can actually be observed.

In any case the theory of lags or leads would seem to be a mere corollary of theories that could explain differences in the structural parameters or in the initial conditions of a dynamic system.

12. THE RÔLE OF 'INITIAL CONDITIONS'

In discussing the parametric family of solutions of (9. 5)–(9.8), we have made a point of distinguishing between the structural parameters and those that describe the starting conditions of the system, the 'initial conditions'. The justification for this distinction is, however, not quite as obvious as it may appear, or as suggested in much of the current literature on economic dynamics.

Among many economists working in the field of dynamic models, a peculiar idea seems to prevail, viz. that the initial conditions of a dynamic system are in a sense theoretically 'less important', or less interesting, than the structural properties of the model. This idea probably derives from the study of simple linear systems, where all members of the particular family of solutions obtained by varying only the initial conditions have something economically interesting in common, e.g. the same period of oscillation, or the same degree of damping per unit of time, etc. The importance of these characteristics derives from a special interest in business cycle theories and from particular views regarding the objective and method of such theories.

Mathematically, the distinction between the structural coefficients of a system and its initial conditions is in fact rather arbitrary. Consider e.g. a simple theory of capital growth, given by

$$\dot{K}(t) = aK(t) + b. \tag{12.1}$$

This equation is said to have as its *general solution* the family of functions obtained by varying the 'arbitrary' constant A in the formula

$$K(t) = Ae^{at} - \frac{b}{a}. \tag{12.2}$$

The parameters a and b the economist would call 'structural coefficients' while A would be 'only an arbitrary constant' to be determined by the initial conditions, e.g. by $A - \frac{b}{a} = K(0) =$ some known number. The constant A is termed arbitrary because it did not appear in the 'law' (12.1).

However, from (12.1) we can derive $\ddot{K} = a\dot{K}$, $\dddot{K} = a\ddot{K}$, and hence, in general,

$$\frac{\dddot{K}}{\ddot{K}} - \frac{\ddot{K}}{\dot{K}} = 0, \text{ or } \frac{d}{dt}\left(\frac{\ddot{K}}{\dot{K}} \right) = 0. \tag{12.3}$$

Here there are no structural coefficients! Still (12.2) is obviously a parametric family of solutions of (12.3). On the other hand, the

57

'general' solution of (12. 3), contains three arbitrary parameters if we use the same terminology as above. Why not say that the economic 'law' is given by (12. 3) and that there are three arbitrary parameters to be determined by the initial conditions, e.g. $K(0)$, $\dot{K}(0)$ and $\ddot{K}(0)$? In fact, we could have many more 'arbitrary' parameters to be determined by 'initial conditions' if we were to consider as the economic 'law' the differential equation obtained by repeated differentiation of (12. 3).

Obviously, the answer to the question of a fundamental distinction between structural parameters and initial conditions is not that of logical or mathematical necessity. The justification for the distinction is based on a known or felt difference in 'meaning' of the two kinds of parameters, in terms of realities that the theory is supposed to describe and explain. The structural parameters are regarded as certain absolute invariants within a class of phenomena, a class deduced by some general principle of reasoning, and within which we are convinced that we shall find the particular phenomenon which we want to 'explain'. The structural parameters, when assumed known, determine this class. We call them the *data of the theory*. Initial conditions are then simply some additional information that is required to identify a particular member of the theoretically deduced class. To illustrate: If we know that the compound interest rate is 4 per cent per year, we can deduce that any investment on this basis will double the original capital in about $17\frac{1}{2}$ years. But if somebody asks how much money he would then have, he would have to tell us how much he wants to invest.

Structural parameters of an explanatory theory are then simply certain properties, which supposedly have a counterpart in real life, and which we think are common to a great many, otherwise different, phenomena.

If we attempt to explain a particular type of evolution (e.g. with regard to capital accumulation), we may think that certain aspects of this evolution are more 'strange' than others. We may concentrate our theoretical efforts upon explaining these particular aspects. The parameters of the theory constructed for this purpose we would call structural parameters. But the strange aspects may be anything, from a complete picture of the time series involved

58

to more vague statements about increases or decreases. It is, therefore, quite obvious that the distinction between 'structural parameters' and 'initial condition' is only a question of how specific an answer we demand from our theory.

A practical counterpart to the procedure of admitting arbitrary initial conditions in our theories is the fact that very often we consider it unnecessary, or hopeless, to explain how a process 'got started'. But we demand to know why it subsequently followed a particularly interesting pattern. In comparative dynamics of the kind that is our subject here it is, however, necessary to pay special attention to the initial conditions and their effect upon the subsequent developments.

We may have the ambition of explaining how the initial conditions are themselves determined, or we may dodge this question. But in any case it is evident from the models previously considered that differences in the initial conditions of two otherwise similar systems may be a source of dissimilarities in the evolution of the two systems. From the study of simple models in Part II we can already single out some characteristic types of dissimilarities that can be produced in this way.

In the systems that have simple exponential solutions, the initial conditions enter as factors of proportionality. If we have two regional economies that are described by the same structural system of this kind, but which have different initial conditions, the dissimilarities in their developments will be very simple. Thus, if they are both expanding, one of the regions will develop uniformly faster than the other. The initial conditions may also differ in such a way that one economy is expanding while the other is contracting. But if both systems move exponentially toward a stationary level this level will *not* depend on the initial conditions and will, therefore, be the same for both regions.

In other systems having more complicated solutions (e.g. the model 6. 4) the effects of changing the initial conditions are in a sense more 'profound'. Even if the structural coefficients are kept constant, changes in the initial conditions may here change a tendency towards stagnation to a tendency towards expansion. The solutions may be stable for some values of the intial conditions, and unstable for other values. In one of the models that we have considered (7. 2) the stationary solution of the system depends on the values of the initial conditions.

Of particular interest is the connection between the values of the initial conditions and the *asymptotic properties* of the system. We can here register the following possibilities, with respect to changes in the initial conditions, the structural parameters being given:

A. The system has one and only one stationary solution.

Then the general class of solutions generated by the initial conditions may be subdivided into the class of stable solutions and the class of unstable solutions (either one of which might be empty).

The asymptotic properties of the solutions in the stable class do not depend on the initial conditions (unless the stationary solution itself depends on initial conditions). That is, if two economies in such a system have different initial conditions they will, if they belong to the stable class, gradually approach the same stationary level.

B. The system has several stationary solutions.

Then the general class of solutions generated by the initial conditions may be subdivided into several classes, some consisting of stable solutions, others of unstable solutions. (A class of this kind may be empty). According to the values of the initial conditions a solution may fall into one or the other of the stable classes, or into an unstable class. Two economies described by such a system may, therefore, show widely different patterns of evolution depending on their respective initial conditions.

C. The system has no stationary solution.

Even in this case some of the members of the class of general solutions may be stable, others unstable. (In case of stability the solutions will here move towards a constant level, an asymptote, which is itself not a solution of the system).

These considerations suggest that two economies which differ 'only' with regard to initial conditions may be very dissimilar in their evolutionary patterns. This conclusion is of course not at all astonishing. The real question is whether it is possible to derive

60

a general dynamic system such that it could be made to fit the development of any region merely by adjusting the initial conditions. Furthermore, we would have to agree that the differences in the initial conditions *do not need any 'explanation'*. We could then perhaps say that we had found a 'cause' of evolutionary dissimilarities: The differences in initial conditions.

It should be noted that the differences in the initial conditions we have been talking about do not mean the same as differences due to dissimilar natural conditions of the various regions. The differences in natural resources, in climate, in racial characteristics etc. are assumed to be included among the *structural* parameters. The initial conditions are the result of some evolutionary process that has taken place in the regions *before* the time from which the dynamic model is assumed to be valid.

Suppose we have two regions that are similar as far as the natural resources, racial characteristics, etc., are concerned. And suppose that, from a certain point of time t_o, both regions develop according to some system of the type (9. 1)–(9.4) but that their initial conditions, e.g. $N(t_o)$, $K(t_o)$ and $S(t_o)$ were different. How could such differences in the initial conditions arise? As already suggested, the differences would have to be the result of some dissimilarity in the paths of development during time preceding t_o. It may even be possible to indicate more specifically how such 'pre-historic' dissimilarities could arise.

For this purpose let us assume that, from a given historic date t_o, the economies of the two regions are described by two identical systems of the type (9. 1)–(9. 4). Thus, all the parameters a, β, γ, δ have exactly the same values for both regions. Assume, for the sake of illustration, that the general parametric family of solutions generated by the initial conditions $N(t_o)$, $K(t_o)$ and $S(t_o)$ can be subdivided into two non-empty classes of which one contains only stable solutions, the other only unstable solutions. We are interested in the case where one of the regions will follow a path belonging to the first class while that of the other region will belong to the second class.

For this purpose let us think of the structural parameters describing behavior as expressing some optimal mode of action under given circumstances. And let us assume that this ability of an

61

optimal mode of action is not something that the people in the two regions were 'born with', but that it is an ability which is *acquired*, in some way or other, during 'pre-historic' time $t < t_o$. The process through which this ability is aquired may have been one of trial and error. It does not seem difficult to visualize that this pre-historic process may have followed different patterns in approaching the identical systems valid from t_o on. We could think of the process as if the system (9. 1)–(9. 4) had been valid also for pre-historic time but with variable parameters converging — in a different way for each region — upon the common, constant, structural parameters valid for $t \geq t_o$. Differences in the 'pre-historic' processes here described would in general lead to *different initial conditions* $N(t_o)$, $K(t_o)$, $S(t_o)$ for the two regions. In particular, the 'pre-historic' processes may lead to such differences in initial conditions that the 'historic' development, for $t \geq t_o$, of one of the regions falls into the class of stable solutions, while that of the other region falls into the class of unstable solutions.

To phrase this proposition in somewhat bolder terms: By the time (here t_0 for both regions) when the two regions have been in operation sufficiently long and have gained enough experience to know what actions correspond to optimal behavior under given environments, they may already during the preceding process of trial and error *have created very different environments* in which to begin at $t = t_o$.

The point is that the processes that we are discussing here are in a sense irreversible. For example, once a region has reached a state of overpopulation, meaning a small amount of capital and low production per head, this case cannot very easily be remedied by a sudden reduction in the size of the population. And the fact that the 'environments' are historically given at any point of time may be an obstacle to improving the environments even in the long run.

To put the hypothesis of dissimilarities due to different initial conditions in still a different way one could perhaps say that 'one region may have become wise before it got stuck,' while the other region 'got stuck before it got wise'. But we have probably here stretched the interpretation of a formal difference a little too far. However, in Part VI we shall have occasion to return to the points that have been mentioned, to give, it is hoped, some more arguments supporting the tentative conclusions hinted at above.

Reviewing the various possibilities that we have now discussed, of explaining interregional dissimilarities by means of rigid dynamic models, we find that there is no particular difficulty in pointing to formal reasons for such dissimilarities. But, at the same time we have found that 'explanations' based on these formal reasons often beg the question in an uncomforting manner. Even in the instances where the 'explanation' may sound somewhat more satisfying, the statements concerning human behavior tend to become too hard-boiled. And the resulting paths of development tend to be too rigid for us to have much confidence in the idea that our model framework could adequately describe the shifting picture — even in the broadest macro terms — of actual economic developments. It is, therefore, desirable to look for other theoretical frameworks that could be more satisfactory in this respect.

The obvious idea of generalization is the introduction of stochastic elements that could make our models and the conclusions we derive from them more flexible. In part IV we shall study some of the possibilities of this approach.

IV. THE STOCHASTIC APPROACH

13. THE NOTION OF RANDOM SHOCKS

Exact models of the type we have been discussing belong, of course, to the world of fiction. Nobody expects such models to depict accurately the facts that we aim to 'explain'. If exact models are to be of practical value, it must be possible to add to them some reasonable interpretation of the deviations between the theory and the facts. Of the various ideas that could serve this purpose we may mention three that are being used very frequently:

a) Ascribing the deviations to 'wrong data', and 'errors of measurement'. If this idea is to mean anything besides the trivial identity that 'facts minus theory equals deviations', it must be possible to describe the would-be 'correct' data, in terms of some technique of observation. In social and economic statistics it is usually not difficult to point out shortcomings of the data at hand and to suggest methods of improvement. However, there is little reason to believe that such improvements would actually close the gap between an exact model and the factual observations. Nevertheless, the notion of 'errors of measurement', etc., may be helpful as a starting point for making assumptions concerning the *nature of deviations* that we consider admissible in connection with a good theory.

b) The notion of an 'incomplete theory because of factors omitted'. The idea here is that real phenomena actually behave according to some exact model, but that such a model would be hopelessly complicated. Therefore, we have to be satisfied with approximations, including only the most important of a possible infinity of explanatory variables. We may not be able even to name all the missing variables, but we may think it possible to make some general statement concerning the nature of errors produced by the omitted factors.

c) The idea that 'the assumption of exact laws is empirically

64

meaningless'. The argument here is that, although it would be convenient if we could reduce the number of degrees of freedom in the world of observations by true statements of the kind: 'If A, then always B', there is no a priori reason why there should exist such a possibility. On the contrary, it may be necessary, from the very beginning, to think in terms of more flexible 'relationships' than those involved in an exact, deterministic model. The rôle of exact models in such a theoretical framework could be that of a partial description of certain aspects of a more complete model.

No matter which of these views one thinks the more fruitful, they point to the necessity of adding new and different theoretical concepts to those occurring in the exact models. A simple, and at the same time promising, idea in this connection is that of including specified stochastic elements in the theories considered. Such stochastic elements may be thought of as representing 'nuisance factors' in a theory designed to establish certain exact and rigorous 'laws'. But the stochastic elements may also be thought of as describing the various constellations of facts that are considered consistent with the general ideas of a particular, exact theory.

The specification of the stochastic elements and their place in the model may depend on which of the above-mentioned points of view the generalized model is based on. But one of the effects will be common to all such 'randomized'' theories, viz. that the statements of exact relationships are changed into statements concerning a joint probability law of the variables considered.

In the case of dynamic models the natural and more realistic counterpart of an exact model is the notion of *stochastic processes*. In dynamic economic models the random elements involved are often called 'shocks'. The terminology is borrowed from mechanics and suggests that the random elements could be considered as exogenous forces affecting an otherwise smooth course of development of the endogenous variables. In a model containing random elements the corresponding 'exact' model might be defined as the model obtained by putting all the random elements identically equal to zero. However, there are other ways of defining the 'exact' part of the model, e.g. by replacing some of the stochastic variables involved by their mathematical expectations. The result thus obtained may be different from that obtained by setting all error terms equal to zero.

The interpretation of the random element as shocks from the 'outside' seems to be linked up especially with the idea mentioned under b) above, viz. that deviations from an exact theory are the result of omitting variables in an otherwise exact model. But the shocks could also be thought of as sudden internal explosions in some of the factors actually included in an exact model, e.g. in some parameters that are assumed to be constant in the exact model.

The factual interpretation of shocks in a dynamic economic model is sometimes rather problematic. In particular, there is the question whether phenomena that we call shocks should rightly be thought of as coming from the outside or whether they should not rather be considered as produced by the economic mechanism considered. In dynamic economics the shocks are often exemplified by such happenings as wars, new technological discoveries, the appearance of leading personalities, spiritual revolutions, and the like. In addition, we have outbursts of epidemic diseases, there is the weather, and we have earthquakes and other catastrophies of nature. On the basis of a philosophy compatible with 'the materialistic interpretation of history' many of these things ought perhaps to be regarded as endogenous factors of a theory of evolution. One would like to single out as shocks only those things that are really independent forces. However, the possibility of such a fundamental and satisfactory concrete distinction between internal and external factors is probably wishful thinking. We may have to choose the less ambitious approach of simply assuming that there are external forces of a certain specified stochastic nature. We may judge the assumption indirectly by the results produced in the way of a reasonably accurate description of actual observations.

A list of factual 'events' that could produce disturbances in an evolutionary system would cover an endless variety of things. One could probably point out disturbing events at each and every moment in history. In fact, at each and every moment one could propably point out a variety of events, some pulling in one direction, some in the opposite direction. It becomes an analytical problem to study whether the *net* effect of a large number of such forces could actually amount to significant distortions of an otherwise smooth path of development.

14. SOME OBSERVATIONS
ON THE USE OF DISCRETE STOCHASTIC PROCESSES

In the simple models frequently used in economic dynamics time is often — artificially — regarded as a sequence of discrete, equidistant points. The economic variables considered (e.g. prices, volume of production, etc.) are then often defined only for equidistant points of time. Sometimes the variables are assumed to remain constant, or to behave in some other prescribed 'regular' manner, over the time interval between two equidistant points. Thus, for example, if $y(t)$ is some economic time series, a set of simple economic assumptions may lead to the statement that

$$y(t) = ay(t-1) + a_o, \ t = 1, 2, \ldots \tag{14.1}$$

where a and a_o are structural constants (or functions of such constants). If the 'lag' involved has economic significance, it can be put equal to 1 as above only by an appropriate choice of unit in which time is measured. If $y(o)$ is given, the formula (14 1) gives the value of $y(t)$, successively, for $t = 1, 2$, etc. The solution of (14.1) has the form

$$y(T) = Aa^T + B, \ T = 1, 2, \ldots \tag{14.2}$$

where $B = \frac{a_o}{1-a}$ and where A is determined by $y(o) = A + B$.

Suppose now that the variable $y(t)$ is subject to random disturbances, $u(t)$, occurring at $t = 1, 2, \ldots$, and entering the system (14.1) in the following way, *

$$y(t) = ay(t-1) + a_o + u(t), \ t = 1, 2, \ldots. \tag{14.3}$$

---

* It will be observed that, in the present section, we use the same symbol $y(t)$ in several different 'meanings', that is, to denote several, alternative processes. I do not think that this typographical simplification should lead to any serious confusion.

We assume, for simplicity, that $u(o) = 0$. It is easy to verify that the value of $y(T)$ for $T \geq 1$ is given by

$$y(T) = Aa^T + B + \sum_{\tau=0}^{T-1} a^\tau u(T-\tau), \ T = 1, 2, \ldots . \quad (14.4)$$

If the random variables $u(t)$, $t = 1, 2, \ldots$ are assumed to be stochastically independent with zero means and constant variance, σ^2, independent of t, the deviations between the 'exact" part of $y(T)$ as given by (14. 2) and the actual value of $y(T)$ as given by (14.4) have, for $a^2 \neq 1$, the variance

$$\sigma^2_{y(T)} = \sigma^2 \sum_{\tau=0}^{T-1} a^{2\tau} = \sigma^2 \frac{1-a^{2T}}{1-a^2}, \ T = 1, 2, \ldots . \quad (14.5)$$

In the formula above it has been assumed that also the *observations* of the series $y(t)$ take place only at $t = 1, 2, \ldots$. But clearly there are many cases where observations may be possible at intermediary points of time (while, of course, the economically significant 'lag' ($= 1$) remains the same). Suppose that the formula (14. 1) is valid for every value of $t \geq 1$. If, in particular, observations were made at intervals of length $= \frac{1}{n}$, we could specify the formula (14. 1) as follows:

$$y\left(t + \frac{i}{n}\right) = ay\left(t + \frac{i}{n} - 1\right) + a_o, \begin{cases} t = 1, 2, \ldots, \\ i = 0, 1, 2, \ldots, n-1. \end{cases} \quad (14. 1. a)$$

The general solution of (14. 1. a), viz.

$$y\left(T + \frac{i}{n}\right) = A_i a^T + B, \begin{cases} T = 1, 2, \ldots \\ i = 0, 1, 2, \ldots, n-1, \end{cases} \quad (14. 2. a)$$

where A_i is determined by the value of $y\left(\frac{i}{n}\right)$, would coincide with (14. 2) for $i = 0$.

Suppose now that there are shocks of the same nature as before, but occurring at points of time $= 1, 1 + \frac{1}{n}, 1 + \frac{2}{n}, \ldots, 2, 2 + \frac{1}{n}, 2 + \frac{2}{n}, \ldots$. The formula (14. 3) is then changed into

$$y\left(t + \frac{i}{n}\right) = ay\left(t + \frac{i}{n} - 1\right) + a_o + u\left(t + \frac{i}{n}\right) \begin{cases} i = 0, 1, 2, \ldots n-1, \\ t = 1, 2, \ldots. \end{cases}$$
$$(14. 3. a)$$

The formula corresponding to (14. 4) then becomes

$$y\left(T + \frac{i}{n}\right) = A_i a^T + B + \sum_{\tau=0}^{T-1} a^\tau u\left(T + \frac{i}{n} - \tau\right), \begin{cases} i = 0, 1, 2, \ldots, n-1, \\ T = 1, 2, \ldots \end{cases}$$
(14. 4.a)

where τ runs over integers $0, 1, 2, \ldots, T-1$.
And, corresponding to (14. 5), we have

$$= \sigma^2 \sum_{\tau=0}^{T-1} a^{2\tau}, \begin{cases} i = 0, 1, 2, \ldots, n-1, \\ T = 1, 2, \ldots \end{cases}$$
(14. 5.a)

Thus, no matter how frequently the shocks occur, if their variance remains the same, the variance $\sigma^2_{y(T)}$ remains the same, and $\sigma^2_{y(t)}$ is constant for $T \leq t < T + 1$.

However, if there are sizeable shocks occurring 'all the time', it may be unreasonable to assume that the ordinate of $y(t)$ should be directly influenced only by the shock occurring at that time. Suppose that all the shocks that have occurred during the lag period from $t - 1$ to t release their effect upon $y(t)$ at t. We should then have

$$y(t) = a y(t-1) + a_o + \sum_{i=1}^{n} u\left(t - 1 + \frac{i}{n}\right), t = 1, 2, \ldots \quad (14. 6)$$

The solution corresponding to (14. 4) would then be

$$y(T) = A a^T + B + \sum_{\tau=0}^{T-1} a^\tau \sum_{i=1}^{n} u\left(T - 1 - \tau + \frac{i}{n}\right), T = 1, 2, \ldots$$
(14. 7)

If the shocks are independent with zero means and have the same variance σ^2 as above, the variance corresponding to (14. 5) will now be

$$\sigma^2_{y(T)} = n\sigma^2 \sum_{\tau=0}^{T-1} a^{2\tau}, T = 1, 2, \ldots. \quad (14. 8)$$

If σ^2 is constant, independent of n, the variance defined by (14. 8) goes to ∞ as $n \to \infty$.

The result may be quite different if we assume that the size of the shocks decreases as their number increases. Suppose for example that we have shocks $u^*(t) = \frac{1}{n} u(t)$, such that

69

$$y(t) = ay(t-1) + a_o + \sum_{i=1}^{n} u^* \left(t - 1 + \frac{i}{n} \right), \qquad (14.9)$$

where the shocks u^* are assumed to be independent with zero means and the same variance $\frac{1}{n^2} \sigma^2$. Then the variance corresponding to (14.5) becomes

$$\sigma^2{}_{y(T)} = \frac{1}{n} \sigma^2 \sum_{\tau=0}^{T-1} a^{2\tau}, \quad T = 1, 2, \ldots, \qquad (14.10)$$

which approaches zero as $n \to \infty$.

If, alternatively, we assume that the shocks u^* are proportional in size to $\frac{1}{\sqrt{n}}$, the corresponding variance of $y(T)$ is independent of the frequency with which the shocks occur.

Thus, if it is reasonable to assume that shocks occur 'all the time', it appears to be very important to decide whether they have a cumulative effect and if so, what assumption should be made concerning their variance.

This fact is brought out more clearly if we consider stochastic *differential* equations, such as those suggested by our simple models of economic growth.

Let us consider the simple differential equation

$$\dot{y}(t) = ay(t) + a_o, \text{ (a and a_o constants, $a \neq 0$)} \qquad (14.11)$$

the solution of which is

$$y(t) = \left(A + \frac{a_o}{a} \right) e^{at} - \frac{a_o}{a}, \qquad (14.12)$$

where A is a constant of integration. Let us disregard the original equation (14.11) for a moment and concentrate upon the function (14.12). If we want to introduce external disturbances acting on the function $y(t)$ this can be done by various principles. One possibility is the following: Assume that when a shock occurs at time t, it does not immediately change the ordinate $y(t)$, (because of a certain amount of 'inertia', as for example in the case where y represents total physical capital in a society). But the shock may be assumed to affect, in an abrupt manner, the *direction* of development at t. $y(t)$ itself will still be a continuous function of

70

time. One way of expressing this principle is to assume that each shock has a lasting influence upon the parameter a_o. We assume, for the sake of simplicity, that the shocks occur at equidistant points of time $t = 1, 2, \ldots$ Denoting the corresponding shocks by $u_1, u_2, \ldots$ the result can be described as follows (when restricting T to *positive integers only*, and assuming $u_o = 0$) [1]

$$y(T) = \left(\left(A + \frac{a_o}{a}\right) e^{aT} - \frac{a_o}{a}\right) + \left(\frac{u_1}{a} e^{a(T-1)} - \frac{u_1}{a}\right) + \ldots +$$

$$+ \left(\frac{u_{T-1}}{a} e^a - \frac{u_{T-1}}{a}\right) = \left[\left(A + \frac{a_o}{a}\right) e^{aT} - \frac{a_o}{a}\right] +$$

$$+ \frac{1}{a} \left[\sum_{\tau=0}^{T-1} u_\tau (e^{a(T-\tau)} - 1) \right], T = 1, 2, \ldots \qquad (14.\,13)$$

If the *u's* are independent with zero means and have the same variance σ^2, the variance of $y(T)$ is given by

$$\sigma^2_{y(T)} = \frac{\sigma^2}{a^2} \left[(T-1) - 2\frac{e^{a(T-1)}-1}{1-e^{-a}} + \frac{e^{2a(T-1)}-1}{1-e^{-2a}} \right], T = 1, 2, \ldots$$
$$(14.\,14)$$

Let us now consider what kind of 'stochastic differential equation' this process corresponds to. Let $\beta(t)$ be a function of time defined in the following manner,

$$\beta(t) \equiv a_o, \; 0 \leq t < 1,$$
$$\beta(t) \equiv a_o + u_1 + u_2 + \ldots + u_j, \; j \leq t < j+1, j = 1, 2, \ldots \qquad (14.\,15)$$

And consider the differential equation

$$\dot{y}(t) = ay(t) + \beta(t), \; t \geq 0 \qquad (14.\,16)$$

The solution of (14. 16) is

$$y(t) = e^{at} \int_0^t \beta(\tau)e^{-a\tau}d\tau + Ae^{at}, \qquad (14.\,17)$$

provided $\frac{dy}{dt}$ is defined as a *right*-hand side derivative at $t = 0, 1, 2,$ etc. A is a constant of integration.

[1] In the following it will be sufficient for our purpose to consider only integral values of t (denoted by T). This simplifies our formulae considerably, as we do not have to deal with shocks the effect of which have lasted only for a fraction of the equidistant time intervals considered.

By integrating step-by-step in (14. 17) it is readily verified that the result is identical with the right hand side of (14. 13) for $t = T =$ any positive integer. The stochastic differential equation (14. 16), therefore, generates exactly the stochastic process described above in connection with the explicit formula (14. 13).

Suppose now that shocks $u(t)$ occur at more frequent intervals. Assume that the function $\beta(t)$ is of the following form

$$\beta(t) \equiv a_o, \ 0 \le t < \frac{1}{n},$$

$$\beta(t) \equiv a_o + u\left(\frac{1}{n}\right) + u\left(\frac{2}{n}\right) + \ldots + u\left(\frac{j}{n}\right), \frac{j}{n} \le t < \frac{j+1}{n}, j = 1, 2, \ldots.$$

(14. 17) will still be the solution of (14. 16), provided the derivatives $\frac{dy}{dt}$ at $t = 0, \frac{1}{n}, \frac{2}{n}$, etc. are defined as *right*-hand side derivatives. From the formula (14. 17) we then have, by integrating step by step up to an integer $t = T$,

$$y(T) = \left(A + \frac{a_o}{a}\right)e^{aT} - \frac{a_o}{a} + \frac{1}{a}\left[\sum_{i=1}^{Tn-1} u\left(\frac{i}{n}\right)\left(e^{a\left(T - \frac{i}{n}\right)} - 1\right)\right], T = 1, 2, \ldots. \tag{14. 18}$$

Assume that the u's are independent with zero means and the same variance σ^2. Then, as n increases the variance of $y(T)$ increases and goes towards infinity when $n \to \infty$. To see this it is sufficient to consider e.g. $y(1)$. The corresponding variance is

$$\sigma^2_{y(1)} = \frac{\sigma^2}{a^2}\sum_{i=1}^{n-1}(e^{a\left(1 - \frac{i}{n}\right)} - 1)^2 \tag{14. 19}$$

This variance obviously approaches infinity with increasing n, since e.g. half of the elements in the sum each have a finite value.

In order that the variance (14. 19) should remain finite it would be necessary to assume that σ^2 decreases as n increases, approaching zero when $n \to \infty$ and such that the right hand side of (14. 19) remains finite. It may be difficult to find concrete reasons for such an assumption.

Let us now consider shocks acting upon the mechanism (14. 11) in a different way. We now assume that the impressed force, which shock represents, ceases to act after a certain time, the continued effect of it after that time being only what it has already done to displace the position of the series y. For simplicity we assume that each shock is in force exactly one unit of time and is then replaced by another shock. The effect after T units of time can then be described by the following expression (when $u_o = 0$),

$$y(T) = \left(A + \frac{a_o}{a}\right) e^{aT} - \frac{a_o}{a} + \frac{1}{a} u_1 (1 - e^{-a}) e^{a(T-1)} + \ldots +$$

$$+ \frac{1}{a} u_{T-1} (1 - e^{-a}) e^a = \left(A + \frac{a_o}{a}\right) e^{aT} - \frac{a_o}{a} +$$

$$+ \frac{1}{a} (1 - e^{-a}) \sum_{\tau=0}^{T-1} u_\tau e^{a(T-\tau)}, \quad T = 1, 2, \ldots \qquad (14.\ 20)$$

If the random variables u are independent with zero means and have the same variance σ^2, the variance of $y(T)$ is given by

$$\sigma^2_{y(T)} = \frac{\sigma^2}{a^2} \frac{1 - e^{-a}}{1 + e^{-a}} (e^{2a(T-1)} - 1'), \quad T = 1, 2, \ldots \qquad (14.\ 21)$$

Consider now the differential equation (14. 16) when $\beta(t)$ is defined in the following manner:

$$\beta(t) \equiv a_o, \ 0 \leq t < 1,$$
$$\beta(t) \equiv a_o + u_j, \ j \leq t < j + 1, \ j = 1, 2, \ldots \qquad (14.\ 22)$$

The solution (14. 17) for integral values T of t then takes the form (14. 20). Hence, the differential equation (14.16) with the specification (14. 22) represents precisely the scheme of shocks leading to (14. 20), with the variance (14. 21).

Here again we want to investigate what happens when the shocks occur at more frequent intervals. For this purpose we now specify the function $\beta(t)$ as

$$\beta(t) \equiv a_o, \ 0 \leq t < \frac{1}{n},$$
$$\beta(t) \equiv a_o + u\left(\frac{j}{n}\right), \ \frac{j}{n} \leq t < \frac{j+1}{n}, \ j = 1, 2, \ldots . \qquad (14.\ 23)$$

The solution corresponding to (14. 20) then becomes

$$y(T) = \left(A + \frac{a_o}{a}\right) e^{aT} - \frac{a_o}{a} +$$

$$+ \frac{1}{a} \left(1 - e^{-\frac{a}{n}}\right) \sum_{i=1}^{Tn-1} u\left(\frac{i}{n}\right) e^{a\left(T - \frac{i}{n}\right)}, \quad T = 1, 2, \ldots . \qquad (14.\ 24)$$

Assume that the u's are independent with the same variance σ^2. And consider the variance of $y(T)$. We have

$$\sigma^2_{y(T)} = \frac{\sigma^2}{a^2}(1 - e^{-\frac{a}{n}})^2 \sum_{i=1}^{Tn-1} e^{2a\left(T-\frac{i}{n}\right)} =$$

$$= \frac{\sigma^2}{a^2}\frac{1-e^{-\frac{a}{n}}}{1+e^{-\frac{a}{n}}}(e^{2a\frac{Tn-1}{n}} - 1),\ T = 1, 2, \ldots. \quad (14.25)$$

This variance obviously approaches *zero* as n goes to infinity, provided σ^2 remains finite.

We shall study the meaning of stochastic differential equations from yet another angle. Let us write

$$\dot{y}(t) = ay(t) + u(t) \quad (14.26)$$

where a is a constant and $u(t)$ a random variable for 'every value of t' and where $u(t_1)$ and $u(t_2)$ are independent for every t_1 and t_2 provided $t_1 \neq t_2$. Assume further that $Eu(t) = 0$ for every t and that the variance σ^2 of $u(t)$ is constant, independent of t.

In order to give precise meaning to the equation (14.26) we consider it as a limiting case of the difference equation

$$\frac{y(t + \Delta t) - y(t)}{\Delta t} = ay(t) + u(t + \Delta t), \quad (14.27)$$

where Δt is arbitrary but fixed > 0, and where $u(t)$ now is a discrete process. The equation (14.27) can be written

$$y(t + \Delta t) = (1 + \Delta ta)y(t) + \Delta t\, u(t + \Delta t). \quad (14.27.a)$$

We put $\Delta t = \frac{1}{n}$, and assume that $y(o)$ is *given*. The solution of the difference equation can then be written as

$$y(T) = \left(1 + \frac{a}{n}\right)^{Tn} y(o) + \frac{1}{n}\sum_{i=0}^{Tn-1} u\left(T - \frac{i}{n}\right)\left(1 + \frac{a}{n}\right)^i,\ T = 1, 2, \ldots.$$
$$\quad (14.28)$$

The variance of $y(T)$ for $|n + a| \neq n$ is given by

$$\sigma^2_{y(T)} = \frac{\sigma^2}{n^2}\frac{1-\left(1+\frac{a}{n}\right)^{2Tn}}{1-\left(1+\frac{a}{n}\right)^2},\ T = 1, 2, \ldots \quad (14.29)$$

As $n \to \infty$ the first member to the right in (14. 28) approaches $y(o)e^{aT}$. But the *variance* of the second member as given by (14. 29) evidently approaches *zero* as $n \to \infty$.

Thus we reach the conclusion that if the shocks have a finite variance, the limiting value of $y(T)$ as the number of shocks approaches infinity is unaffected by the shocks. The expected value and the variance of the 'effect' are both zero. This result could be changed, e.g. by assuming that the variance of each shock increases proportionally with n. The practical interpretation of such a process may be difficult. [1]

If we may draw any general conclusion from the preceding examples it seems to be this: When the variables u are independent and all have the finite variance σ^2, the cumulated effect upon the variable y during a finite period of time seems to be either zero or infinite. In order to avoid such unrealistic results some 'trick' assumption seems to be necessary concerning the asymptotic behavior of σ^2 when the number of shocks per unit of time increases beyond limits. If the process $\{u(t)\}$ is discrete with only a finite number of shocks in a given time interval, this difficulty does not arise.

Leaving the problem of a realistic choice between these alternatives aside for a moment, let us consider the possibility of approximating an arbitrary, but discrete, process of shocks by assuming equidistant shocks, e.g. one shock at the beginning of each 'year'. It seems that a rather strong justification for such an approximation can be given if we assume that the shock-receiving system *moves slowly*, relative to the unit of time considered. Thus, for example, if we assume that there is only one shock every year but that its exact time of occurrence during the year is arbitrary, we make at most an error of one year's extra 'cumulation' by allocating the shock to the beginning of the year. The long-range effect of this error in a slowly moving evolutionary system is likely to be relatively negligible. Suppose, next, that there are, ordinarily, several shocks during a year, but that their sum has a finite variance. Then it is evident from the formulae considered above that the error of considering the sum of the shocks during a year

[1] Cf. A. Khintchine: Asymptotische Gesetze der Wahrscheinlichkeitsrechnung, Berlin 1933, p. 9, footnote.

as one shock at the beginning of the year may also be negligible, when the system moves slowly.

Thus, if we restrict ourselves to processes $\{u(t)\}$ that are reasonable in the sense that they cause only relatively small *short-time* displacements of the evolutionary variables considered, the simplifying assumption of equidistant (annual) shocks may not be very serious.

The assumptions to be made regarding the stochastic nature of the process $\{u(t)\}$ are more problematic. From the point of view of concrete interpretation the assumption of continuous processes $\{u(t)\}$ does not appear promising, in particular if we want a realistic form of the transformed process $\{y(t)\}$. It is, of course, true that a discrete process $\{u(t)\}$, where the variances are finite, would not always give realistic results either. The assumptions concerning the way in which the system absorbs the shocks here obviously play an important role. However, the assumption of discrete finite shocks seems to go well with a reasonable specification of the manner of absorbtion.

It would seem realistic to define the process $\{u(t)\}$ on the basis of the following considerations: 1) The shocks that matter in a macro process are 'big' shocks. 2) Such shocks may occur *at any time*, but *they do not occur very frequently*. 3) They are stochastically independent. We want to mention a well-known process that seems to meet these requirements, viz. the generalized Poisson process. [1]

Consider a fixed unit of time, e.g. a year. We divide the year into n equal intervals. Assume that in each of these intervals there can be either no shock or one shock, and that the probability of a shock occurring during a particular interval is $= \lambda/n$, where λ is a constant. If a shock does not occur, it is defined to have the value zero. *If* a shock occurs we assume that it takes on values according to a *given probability law*, which is independent of the 'events' in other intervals. Suppose that *if* a shock u_i occurs in the i-th interval, its value has a continuous probability *density* function $p(u_i)$. The probability of a shock $\neq 0$ but $< U$ in a given interval is then

[1] Cf. A. Khintchine. Op. cit. p. 21.

$$P(u_i \leq U \mid u_i \neq 0) = \frac{\lambda}{n} \int\limits_{-\infty}^{U} p(u_i) du_i, \; i = 1, 2, \ldots, n. \qquad (14.\,30).$$

(Since $p(u_i)$ is a density function, it does not matter that we integrate across the excluded point $u = 0$.)

The number of shocks (or, rather, the number of non-zero shocks) k occurring during a whole year is a random variable defined by the distribution

$$p_k = \binom{n}{k} \left(\frac{\lambda}{n}\right)^k \left(1 - \frac{\lambda}{n}\right)^{n-k} \qquad (14.\,31)$$

which, for $n \to \infty$, becomes

$$\lim_{n \to \infty} p_k = \frac{\lambda^k e^{-\lambda}}{k!} \qquad (14.\,32)$$

If $\bar{\sigma}^2$ is the (constant) variance of a shock *when it occurs*, and the shocks are independent, the variance of the *sum*, $u^*(t)$, of all shocks during the year t to $t + 1$ is, for $n \to \infty$,

$$\sigma^2_{u^*(t)} = \bar{\sigma}^2 \sum_{0}^{\infty} k \frac{\lambda^k e^{-\lambda}}{k!} = \lambda \bar{\sigma}^2 \qquad (14.\,33)$$

If we want to use the approximation of 'one shock at the beginning of each year', we could define the annual shocks as the sequence $u^*(t)$. The transformed process $\{y(t)\}$ may, nevertheless, be continuous. But values of $y(t)$ within the same year will be functionally dependent and thus, in a sense, form a 'degenerate' stochastic process.

15. ON THE PARAMETRIC REPRESENTATION OF
RANDOM DISTURBANCES IN MODELS OF ECONOMIC GROWTH

In Section 13 we discussed possible concrete interpretations of random elements acting upon an exact economic model. In Section 14 we gave simple illustrations of various ways in which random disturbances may be 'absorbed' and 'propagated' in a dynamic model. The disturbances were regarded as *external* forces, even though such disturbances might well be produced by the actions of the peoples and institutions whose behavior the models aim to describe. We have talked of the random variables, $u(t)$, as if these quantities were themselves identical with the factual random events that we have called shocks or disturbances.

Actually, it is in some respects a matter of convention how to interprete, in concreto, the random elements of a model. We could assume the relevant random events 'themselves' to be explicit parts of the model, the form of the model determining their way of action. Or, we might assume the model to contain certain random parameters that merely describe the *manner of impact* of some unspecified random event. However, in the preceding section we assumed the quantities $u(t)$ to have a concrete, quantitative meaning. That was the reason that we were concerned about their having e.g. a finite variance and other 'realistic' characteristics. Now, clearly it may be rather difficult to measure the 'size' of a random event 'per se'. To have quantitative meaning the measure must be that of the *effect* that random events have upon something measureable. This brief excursion into philosophy would seem to suggest the conclusion that the variables $u(t)$ ought to be regarded as *variable, descriptive, parameters of the model concerned.* In some cases such parameters may be regarded as the 'receptors' of external shocks.

Choosing this parametric interpretation of 'shocks' let us consider the possibilities of 'randomizing' the dynamic system (9. 1)–(9. 4), (or even the more general system (9. 5)–(9. 8).) We may get some idea of how to make the system stochastic, in a parametric way, by turning the question around, that is, by asking what kind of stochastic model the exact system could be deduced from. Here there are various possibilities. And there are of course also various ways of 'deducing' an exact model from a given stochastic model. We may distinguish between the following — not mutually exclusive — possibilities.

1. The functional forms φ, ψ, f, and g, could be regarded as the 'condensed' form of other functions containing additional parameters of a stochastic nature. The exact function could be considered as the simplified expression obtained by putting certain random parameters equal to zero (i.e. by 'omitting factors').

2. The parameters α, β, γ, δ, might actually be random para-

meters, the exact model being obtained by approximating these parameters by some constants.

3. The quantities to the left in the equations (9. 1)–(9. 4) may have to be interpreted, not as the actual observable variables, but as the 'expected value' of these variables, given the values of the observable variables in the right hand sides.

4. More generally, the variables $X(t)$, $N(t)$, $K(t)$, and $S(t)$ in the exact model may have to be interpreted merely as some parametric properties of the stochastic process out of which the corresponding actually observed sequences are a sample. Thus it might be that the system (9. 1)–(9. 4) would be valid only if $X(t)$, $N(t)$, $K(t)$ and $S(t)$ are replaced by $E(X(t))$, $E(N(t))$, $E(K(t))$ and $E(S(t))$, or, by the corresponding 'modes' of the variables, or by some other more complicated parametric properties of the actual stochastic process.

Of these possible assumptions the most simple one would seem to be that the constant parameters a, β, γ, δ represent *expected values* substituted for an exactly corresponding set of random parameters, and that there are no other random parameters involved. This would mean that the system (9. 1)–(9. 4) could be made directly applicable to the facts simply by re-instituting the parameters a, β, γ, δ as random variables (actually: random processes) possessing certain known stochastic properties. The 'causes' of such stochastic variation of the parameters may e.g. be certain external 'shocks' as discussed above.

The factual interpretation of the parameters a, β, γ, δ was discussed in Section 10. It would seem quite reasonable that they should be subject to changes of a stochastic nature. The question is what kind of stochastic properties we should assume the parameters to have.

If the parameters a, β, γ, δ are assumed to be the expected values of some corresponding random parameters, the stochastic parameters could be written in the form $(a_1 + v_{a_1}(t))$, $(a_2 + v_{a_2}(t))$ etc., where the v's have expected values = zero for each point of time. We have previously tried to justify the assumption that the random events producing the effects v are from a discrete process which may be approximated by assuming 'one shock each year'. The question is then how long the effect due to a particular shock should be assumed to influence the corresponding parameter. In the preceding section we studied two kinds of assumptions concerning the duration of a shock effect. One assumption was that each shock produces an everlasting, constant effect upon the parameters. Another assumption was that the effect of a shock ceases as soon as a new shock occurs. These assumptions probably represent extremes. In the case of parameters describing behavior it is probably reasonable to assume some degree of stability in the sense that the effect of a shock tapers off gradually, e.g. according to a decreasing exponential function.

Systems, even of the simple types discussed in Part II, may become very complicated stochastic processes if all the parameters are assumed to be random. This is true even if we assume very simple stochastic properties of the parameters. But already the simple illustrations in Section 14 are sufficient to show that stochastic elements in an otherwise very elementary evolutionary process may produce an infinity of irregular paths of developments some of which are very different from others.

This conclusion may be true even if the parametric effect of each shock is small as against the average size of the parameter concerned. That the random elements may play a decisive rôle in shaping the paths of development is as obvious as the fact — illustrated in Part II — that widely different paths can be produced by changing the parameters of a particular, exact, system. Take, for instance, the system discussed in 6. 4. Here the initial conditions determine whether there shall be progressive expansion or degeneration towards a possible stationary level. If at a certain point of time a big shock changes the structural parameters, the system may be thrown from a path of expansion to a path that leads to stagnation. The reason for this may be e.g. that the amount of available capital sufficient for progress under certain values of the parameters may not be sufficient under other values of the parameters.

There is no question that the introduction of elementary random elements, even in systems of the simple kind discussed in Part II, could generate random processes of a very realistic nature as far as resemblance to facts is concerned. But we have still to discuss whether this means that we have here reached a possible explanation also with respect to large evolutionary dissimilarities as between several simultaneously existing economic regions.

16. THE RÔLE OF RANDOM ELEMENTS IN PRODUCING EVOLUTIONARY DISSIMILARITIES

In discussing the dissimilarities that could be produced by exact deterministic models we had the simple starting point that if two regions had the same structural system and the same initial conditions their paths of progress would be identical. In a stochastic system the situation is different in the sense that a given stochastic process may give rise to infinitely many different factual paths of development. Therefore, if we have said that the economy of two regions are described by the same stochastic process we have not said that their factual developments will be alike.

The variances $\sigma^2_{y(T)}$ studied in Section 14 measure, in an incomplete fashion, the divergences that could arise between two regions following the same stochastic process, at least in the case where the shocks, u, for the two regions are *stochastically independent*. If this assumption is made, the stochastic formulation implies, as something quite natural, that the various regions should develop differently.

In order that developments in two regions should be identical, the actual shocks (the 'sample' sequence of shocks) would have to be the same and would have to be received in the same manner in the two regions. This means that the shocks affecting the two regions would have to be functionally dependent.

Actually, the realistic assumption is probably, in most cases, something in between these extremes; i.e. if the sequence of shocks for region No. 1 is $u_1(1)$, $u_1(2)$, etc., and for region No. 2 $u_2(1)$, $u_2(2)$, etc., we may expect that simultaneous shocks $u_1(t)$ and $u_2(t)$ would be due, in part at least, to some common, random event. We want to illustrate the effect of such interdependence by means of a very simple model.

Let $y_1(t)$ and $y_2(t)$ denote some economic variable for region

81

no. 1 and region no. 2, respectively. (y may e.g. be 'capital' as in models 6. 2 and 8. 2.) Assume that the 'exact' model is the same for the two regions, e.g. $\dot{y}_1 = ay_1 + a_o$, and $\dot{y}_2 = ay_2 + a_o$ and that $y_1(0) = y_2(0)$. Assume further that the stochastic processes $y_1(t)$ and $y_2(t)$ for the two regions are given by

$$\dot{y}_1(t) = ay_1(t) + \beta_1(t), \tag{16. 1}$$

and
$$\dot{y}_2(t) = ay_2(t) + \beta_2(t), \tag{16. 2}$$
where

$$\beta_1(t) \equiv a_o, \, 0 \leq t < 1 \tag{16. 3}$$

$$\beta_1(t) \equiv a_o + u_1(1) + u_1(2) + \ldots + u_1(n), n \leq t < n+1, n = 1, 2, \ldots,$$
and

$$\beta_2(t) \equiv a_o, \, 0 \leq t < 1, \tag{16. 4}$$

$$\beta_2(t) \equiv a_o + u_2(1) + u_2(2) + \ldots + u_2(n), \, n \leq t < n+1,$$

$$n = 1, 2, \ldots \ldots$$

Assume further that $E(u_1(t))^2 = E(u_2(t))^2 = \sigma^2$, and that $E(u_1(\tau_1)u_2(\tau_2)) = \sigma_{12}$ when $\tau_1 = \tau_2$, and $= 0$ when $\tau_1 \neq \tau_2$, $\tau_1, \tau_2 = = 1, 2, \ldots \ldots$; $Eu_1(t) = Eu_2(t) = 0$; $u_1(0) = u_2(0) = 0$.

We want to calculate the variance of the difference ($y_1(T) - y_2(T)$), where T is a positive integer.

From the formula (14. 13) we have, directly,

$$\sigma^2_{[y_1(T) - y_2(T)]} = \frac{1}{a^2} E \left[\sum_{\tau = 0}^{T-1} u_1(\tau) (e^{a(T-\tau)} - 1) - \sum_{\tau = 0}^{T-1} u_2(\tau)(e^{a(T-\tau)} - 1) \right]^2 =$$

$$= \frac{2(\sigma^2 - \sigma_{12})}{a^2} \left[(T - 1) - 2 \frac{e^{a(T-1)} - 1}{1 - e^{-a}} + \frac{e^{2a(T-1)} - 1}{1 - e^{-2a}} \right]. \tag{16. 5}$$

Thus, if there is perfect, positive correlation between the two series of shocks, we could say, under rather general assumptions, that the probability of any material dissimilarity between the two regions at $t = T$ is equal to zero. The smaller the covariance σ_{12}, the more probable it is that a wide dissimilarity between the two regions will actually materialize.

Returning now to the case where $u_1(t)$ and $u_2(t)$ are independent, there is another conclusion which is obvious from the formula (14. 13): If $a > o$ and if — because of previous shocks —

$y_1(T) > y_2(T)$ this difference can be expected (with a certain probability) *to continue and to increase* with time. If $y_1(T)$ is much larger than $y_2(T)$ because of differences in the previous shocks, the probability that the position of the two regions in the future should be reversed may be small.

There is the possibility that a system may become more 'shock-proof' as it cumulates time of experience. That is, a certain type of shock may be very disturbing during the 'infancy' of a region while gradually the shocks have a smaller and smaller impact upon the parameters affected. If two regions more or less accidentally experienced very different shocks in the 'beginning', while gradually the influence of the shocks tapered off, differences in the early shocks may have caused a permanent — and perhaps widening — gap between the development of the two regions (and more so than in the case of a constant intensity of the shock effects).

Thus it would seem perfectly possible to construct stochastic processes, of a not too complicated type, that could represent irrefutable theories when tested against available data on economic evolution. In fact, the trouble is probably rather that it is almost *too easy* to find 'explanations' in this direction. The resulting stochastic models may not yield very much in the way of significant long-range forecasts. It is, therefore, essential that as much as possible of the 'interesting' aspects of evolution should already be covered by the exact part of the model.

From this point of view we have now to consider the effects of economic contact between several regions.

V. THEORIES OF INTERREGIONAL RELATIONS

17. NATURE OF INTERREGIONAL ACTIVITIES

In our model analyses we have so far paid little attention to interregional economic and social relations. The models we have studied were for a single region. And if we did not impose the condition that the region should be in isolation, we assumed that the effects of contact with other regions could be represented by constant parameters in the one-region model. We have now to consider more explicitly the interactions in a network of regions.

In the field of 'strictly economic' theories the answer to our new question would be a theory of international trade. Here one could e.g. show the opportunities of gains for all regions by an exchange of goods and services. By making appropriate assumptions one could show how the various regions, guided by rational behavior, would establish and maintain peaceful and advantageous commercial intercourse. However, it will probably be admitted that economic theory of international trade has had more success in demonstrating what *could* be — or even what should be — than in explaining what *is* or *has been*. The assumptions of given political conditions, etc., reduce the theory of international trade to some kind of partial analysis. The rôle of such theories in explaining the historical development of interregional relations may not be too great. There are other things that the regions can do — and have done — to each other besides exchanging goods and services.

First, there is the possibility of a natural kind of competition for a share in common, limited resources. By peacefully outgrowing other regions with regard to size of population, one or more regions may deprive others of essential means of subsistence. But the effects could also be the other way round, if there is a pronounced element of complementarity as between scales of activity in the various regions.

Second, there are other means of acquiring goods and services than by production and peaceful trade. One need not think only of brutal grabbing, and exploitation. It is possible to spend potentially productive power not only upon making goods and carrying them, but also — and perhaps with considerable individual success — upon the very methods of trading. Likewise, it may pay for a region to spend potential, productive power upon activities to *prevent* other regions from carrying out transfer operations of the 'something-for-very-little' type. Competition, in economic theory, is usually taken to mean making and offering useful things more efficiently than one's neighbor, or producing for less. Competition *as such* is not assumed to involve effort or waste of resources. However, this means using the term 'competition' in a very timid sense. At any rate, whatever be the terminology chosen, it would seem necessary somehow to recognize as a possibility the use of potentially productive power for other things than what is ordinarily meant by 'production'.

Third, there is the important 'trade' in knowledge, ideas and ideologies. These items have — at least very often — the peculiar and fortunate property that they can be sold and still kept. Were it not for the difficulties of quantitative measurement, one might well hold that 'trade' of this kind has meant more in the process of evolution than all the material goods that have crossed regional borders. On the other hand, one cannot say, without further analysis, whether the element of knowledge has been a factor of homogenization or one that has widened interregional disparities.

Finally, there is the question of human migrations. People moving into a region may exploit the population already there, or their activities may work out to the mutual benefit of both the natives and the settlers. However, as we are here concerned only with macro-theories, for each region as a whole, our theories will show the effects of emigration and immigration only as far as such changes in population affect total (or per capita) output of the regions. As a result of migrations it is e.g. quite possible that both emigrants' regions and immigrants' regions may have more goods and services per capita than before, while the natives of the immigrants' regions have less. It is probably not entirely impossible to indicate some of the main *economic* forces affecting migration. On the other hand, to construct something like a

85

complete explanatory theory is probably a formidable task, perhaps a hopeless one.

In the following sections we shall try to indicate a theoretical framework that takes into account certain aspects of the abovementioned types of interregional activities and interactions. We shall study them one by one, although the final purpose should be to arrive at a model where they all enter. However, reaching for such high goals as those announced here, our modest 'results' below will probably deserve the label of an anticlimax.

18. A MODEL OF 'PEACEFUL' INTERREGIONAL CONTACT

In discussing the production function of a region, we have assumed that the volume of output was uniquely related to the size of population (or more correctly: the size of the working population), the amount of available capital, and the level of know-how. From the point of view of economic theory one could here object that the amount of production depends not only on the labor force but on how hard it works. Economic theory asserts that the input of labor per man depends on remuneration. In economic macro-theories this matter is usually dealt with in a simplified way, by introducing some assumption of constant work hours, or the like. However, if one wants to introduce a more general concept of production than that common in economic theory, the assumption of 'constant intensities' of input may perhaps be justified on a more sophisticated, theoretical basis. The line of thought that we have in mind is this:

Consider a single individual, and consider *all* the activities that he carries out during a day, a year, etc., in order to acquire — directly or indirectly — the products and benefits that he desires. Surely, the activities of an average individual for this purpose cover much more than going to a factory, operating there for eight hours, and then leaving for home. The division between work and leisure is in a sense somewhat arbitrary. At any rate, the distinction is much less sharp than assumed in economic theory for the purpose of deducing the 'supply curve' of labor or similar concepts. From a more general point of view it may in fact be more realistic to assume that the individual is constantly engaged in some activity in his own interest and for his own benefit. He may have a larger or a smaller capacity to carry out such activities, depending on his personal abilities, desires, and ambitions, and on the additional power given to him by available capital equipment and acquired skill and knowledge. But given these latter factors one might quite possibly reach a useful theoretical concept by assuming that the total 'input capacity' of a particular individual is a characteristic constant. One could carry this idea further, into the field of macro-theories. The corresponding notion for a whole economic region would be an index of total input capacity, the level of which would depend on the size of the population, the available amount of capital and the general level of acquired education and know-how.

One could consider total output (previously denoted by X) as an index of total input capacity of a region. However, it seems more promising to introduce the concept of input capacity as an abstract, auxiliary parameter which, in turn, produces tangible result in the form of goods and services. The theoretical scheme that we are aiming at is one where the production function (9. 1) determines, not the final supply of goods and services but the internal *power* of a region to manufacture or acquire goods and services of all kinds. A parameter of this nature may appear as something very abstract and artificial, but actually is no more so than the more common notions of total output, national product, etc. The measurement of such variables is always to some extent a question of inventing more or less artificial indices based on subjective evaluation.

The auxiliary parameter measuring the *input capacity* of a region we shall denote by Y. Let there be M regions in the network considered. And let Y_i correspond to region No. $i, i = 1, 2, \ldots, M$. We shall assume that Y_i is given by a *capacity function*

$$Y_i = \varphi_i(N_i, K_i, S_i), i = 1, 2, \ldots, M, \qquad (18.\ 1)$$

where N, K and S mean population, capital, and an index of education, respectively. We want to use the Y's for the definition of a *global production function* for all the regions taken together. If X measures global output, we assume that it is given by a 'production function'

87

$$X = \Phi(Y_1, Y_2, \ldots, Y_M). \tag{18.2}$$

This global function could be interpreted as follows:

Assume that X is a measure of the value of total production, just like the national product for a single region. The national product of an isolated region is not the sum — in a physical sense — of the quantities of goods and services produced. It is the value of these products after they have been distributed among the members of the region according to some given system of exchange. In the same way we shall interprete X as the global product resulting both from productive activities within each region *and* from trading activities between the regions. In what follows we shall assume that X has a maximum value for each set of values of the variables $Y_i, i = 1, 2, \ldots, M,$ and that this maximum is given by (18.2). This maximum obviously depends on the structure of the interregional market, whether there are many regions or few regions, whether the regions permit 'free trade', etc. We shall here assume that X is a result of a given system of relatively free trading practices between the regions. The more aggresive practices of trade restrictions, hard bargains, etc., will be introduced in a different way, viz. by assuming that such activities affect the net input factors Y_i. This will be considered in the next section. In the present section we shall assume that interregional activities consist only of 'peaceful' exchange of goods and services in a manner to be defined implicitly by the relations described below.

Let X_i be the part of global output that finally belongs to region No. i. The value of X_i will, in general, depend not only on the input capacity Y_i but also on the Y's for the other regions in the system. The principle by which X_i is determined is not something given by nature. Even if all the regions had the same input, Y, it does not follow that they should all get the same share. Whatever be the internal structure of the regions, some additional assumption is required concerning their strategic position in the regional network, in order to deduce the size of the quantities X_i.

We shall assume that this problem of distribution is solved through the existence of a set of characteristic *allotment functions*,

$$X_i = \xi_i(Y_1, Y_2, \ldots, Y_M), i = 1, 2, \ldots, M, \tag{18.3}$$

88

satisfying the identity

$$\sum_{i=1}^{M} \xi_i \equiv \Phi, \tag{18.4}$$

for all values of $Y_1, Y_2, \ldots, Y_M$.

The assumption that (18.4) is an *identity* and not just another equation of the system means an a priori restriction upon the set of admissible allotment functions. We assume, in other words, that *if* a certain global product is somehow brought out, there is a given mechanism by which the allotment takes place so as to exhaust the whole product. (This assumption, of course, does *not* mean that the allotment system does not affect total output.) The alternative assumption, that (18.4) be an *equation* and not an identity would lead us to a whole series of new and, indeed, very interesting theoretical problems in addition to those considered here. More specifically, such an assumption would remove one more degree of freedom from the structural system considered. It is easy to see that this would take us right into the kind of problems discussed in modern short-run theories of 'involuntary unemployment' and 'overproduction'. The justification for leaving out these particular problems in our discussion here is the — perhaps bold — idea that the long-range effects of the short-run phenomena mentioned can be incorporated in the *form* of the functional relations considered.

One might think that e.g. $X_i = \dfrac{\partial \Phi}{\partial Y_i} Y_i$ would be the 'natural share' of region No. i, but such a set of allotment functions would not in general exhaust the global product $X = \Phi$. There is no reason to believe that Φ would be homogeneous of degree 1 in the Y's.

A very simple example of allotment functions that satisfy the requirement (18.4) is the following,

$$X_i = h \frac{Y_i}{\Sigma Y_j} \Phi + h_i \Phi, \; i = 1, 2, \ldots, M, \tag{18.3.a}$$

where h and $h_i, i = 1, 2, \ldots, M$ are constants such that $\sum_1^M h_j = = 1 - h$. This would mean that each region gets a share in proportion to its relative input plus a 'social' share.

89

Equations (18. 1), (18. 3) together with equations of the type (9. 2), (9. 3) and (9. 4) for each region would form a complete set of relations for the regional network. (In equations (9. 2)–(9. 4) we should then have the variables X_i, N_i, K_i and S_i).

If the allotment functions ξ_i and the global production function Φ were of such a nature that X_i would depend only on Y_i, we should in fact be back with a system for each region of the type (9. 1)–(9. 4). But this would not seem to represent a very realistic case. In general, we must assume that the welfare of a region, given its own efforts, will depend essentially on the activities of other regions. These activities may be competing, complementary or a mixture of both. Although, presumably, the exchange of goods between the regions is by itself mutually advantageous, the growth of the variable Y in one region may mean that others get less. That depends on the form of the allotment functions (18. 3).

Suppose, for example, that the allotment functions are of the form (18. 3. a) and that Φ has the extremely simple form

$$X = a \sum_{i=1}^{M} Y_i + a_o \qquad (18.\ 2.\text{a})$$

Then the region No. i would have the share

$$X_i = ha Y_i + ha_o \frac{Y_i}{\sum\limits_{j=1}^{M} Y_j} + h_i a \sum_{j=1}^{M} Y_j + h_i a_o \qquad (18.\ 3.b)$$

We assume here that a, h, and h_i are all positive.

If e.g. Y_j, $(j \neq i)$ in (18. 3. a) increases, the other $(M-1)Y$'s remaining constant, the effects upon X_i are of two kinds. One effect is a decrease in X_i because Y_i now is a smaller relative part of total input. Another effect is an increase in X_i for the reason that there will now be a bigger global product to share. If the region No. i itself increased input Y_i, while the other regions did not, it would increase X_i by increasing its relative competitive position and by creating more goods and services to be shared by everybody.

From the way in which Y_i is assumed to be determined it is obvious that an advantageous allotment function for a particular region can give rise to a more rapid growth of input capacity in that region than in other regions. Such a development may lead to a growing disparity between the regions, even if they have similar structures (9. 2)–(9. 4). On the other hand, regions that for some reason have different structures (9. 2)–(9. 4) may become more similar through mutual trading. The result in this respect again depends on the global production function (18. 2) and on the allotment functions (18. 3) that characterize the mutual contact between the regions.

19. STRATEGIES OF 'GRABBING', PROTECTION AND COOPERATION

In the preceding section the inputs Y_i were assumed to be functions of the variables N_i, K_i, and S_i. Hence, the quantities Y would be fixed quantities at any given moment of time. In this respect the Y's are different from e.g. the notion of 'supply of labor', which generally is assumed to be freely adaptable to the remuneration offered at any time. It is not our idea here to suggest that human decisions to work harder or less hard play no rôle. But we want to bring the element of choice into the picture in a somewhat different manner.

As we have mentioned, the idea that people either produce, in a strictly economic sense, or do nothing, gives a rather incomplete picture of human life. There is the alternative possibility of including under 'production' practically everything that people do, perhaps apart from being asleep. There is, however, a third alternative, viz. to make a distinction between 'productive' and 'unproductive' efforts. We do not here want to raise the old quarrel with the Mercantilists or the Physiocrats, as to what is productive and what is not. We merely want a conceptual framework capable of expressing the indubitable fact that there are other forms of human activities than those usually thought of in economic theories of production. We want to recognize that these other activities may require effort and, therefore, in various ways, compete with production in the more narrow sense. We want to be able to express the fact that 'unproductive' activities may be directed towards actually hampering the productive efforts of other groups.

The idea we want to introduce is that the total input capacity of a region may find an outlet in two directions, one leading to a larger global output of goods and services, another towards securing a larger share in the total. A distinction of this kind has e.g. been suggested by V. Pareto. [1] Abstractions being unavoidable, a conceptual framework based on a simple distinction between these two kinds of activities seems to be somewhat more general and realistic than the other alternatives mentioned above.

Let Y_i' and Y_i'' denote the productive and the unproductive part, respectively, of total input capacity, Y_i. Assuming additivity, we have

$$Y_i' + Y_i'' = Y_i, i = 1, 2, \ldots, M, \qquad (19.1)$$

where Y_i is determined by an equation of the type (18. 1). The global production function (18. 2) will now be defined as

$$X = \Phi(Y_1', Y_2', \ldots, Y_M'). \qquad (19.2)$$

Assume now that, of the total share X_i obtained by region No. i, a part X_i' is obtained by productive activities Y_i', while another part, X_i'', is obtained by unproductive activities Y_i''. We assume as before that X_i' is obtained as the result of an allotment function

$$X_i' = \xi_i'(Y_1', Y_2', \ldots, Y_M'), \qquad (19.3)$$

satisfying

$$\sum_{i=1}^{M} \xi_i' \equiv \Phi, \qquad (19.4)$$

for all values of $Y_1', Y_2', \ldots, Y_M'$.

With regard to the result, X_i'', of the activity Y_i'', it would seem reasonable to assume that X_i'' also depends on how much efforts of this kind the other regions put in, and on how much there is available to fight about. That is, the 'allotment functions' determining the results of the unproductive efforts might perhaps be assumed to be of the type

$$X_i'' = \xi_i''(Y_1'', Y_2'', \ldots, Y_M''; \Phi), \qquad (19.5)$$

and such that

$$\sum_{i=1}^{M} \xi_i'' \equiv 0. \qquad (19.6)$$

for all values of $Y_1'', Y_2'', \ldots, Y_M''$, and Φ.

[1] V. Pareto, Manuel d'économie politique, Paris, 1909, p. 466.

Regarding the nature of the allotment functions (19. 5), it is probably reasonable to assume that

$$\frac{\partial \xi_i''}{\partial Y_i''} > 0, \frac{\partial \xi_i''}{\partial Y_j''} < 0, i \neq j, i = 1, 2, \ldots, M, \qquad (19.7)$$
$$j = 1, 2, \ldots, M.$$

It is perhaps also reasonable to assume that

$$\frac{\partial \xi_i''}{\partial \Phi} > 0, i = 1, 2, \ldots, M. \qquad (19.8)$$

The meaning of $\partial \xi_i''/\partial Y_i''$ being negative is that unproductive activities by one region must be assumed to meet with counter-measures from other regions. The net gain, for a particular region, from this kind of activity is then the result of the efforts that the region can muster over and beyond what it requires to defend itself against the unproductive activities of other regions.

As a very simple illustration of ξ''-functions satisfying the abovementioned formal requirements consider the functions

$$X_i'' = \eta (Y_i'' - b_i \sum_{j=1}^{M} Y_j'') \frac{\Phi}{\sum\limits_{j=1}^{M} Y_j''}, i = 1, 2, \ldots, M, \qquad (19.\,5.a)$$

where η and the b's are positive constants such that $\sum\limits_{i=1}^{M} b_i = 1$. Here the inverse of the factor $\Phi/\Sigma Y_j''$ may be interpreted as the average pressure of the unproductive activities upon the total of goods and services available. The expression $b_i \Sigma Y_j''$ could be interpreted as the efforts of defense necessary for region No. i, in order to 'keep what it has'. If Y_i'' exceeds the necessary defensive efforts, the region will make net gains in the struggle.

The essential observation to be made in connection with the model here presented is that the existence of opportunities (19. 5) must be expected *generally to lead to a reduction in global output*, as compared with the case where all efforts go into the function (19. 2). The question is how much of the total input capacities Y_i will be spent on unproductive activities.

If we assume that there are many regions and that each of them operates alone in trying to grab as much as possible of global riches, we are led to consider equilibrium conditions of the following well-known type:

$$\frac{\partial \xi_i'}{\partial Y_i'} = \frac{\partial \xi_i''}{\partial Y_i''}, \quad i = 1, 2, \ldots, M. \tag{19.9}$$

That is, the 'marginal productivities' in the two directions should be the same. Whether or not the conditions (19. 9) mean a stable solution would depend on the nature of the functions ξ' and ξ''.

In a 'free-for-all' system of the type described there would be two kinds of constraints that could prevent a region from turning all its capacity into pure 'grabbing'' operations. One constraint would be the fact that it usually is more profitable to spend at least some effort in the direction of creative production. Another constraint is the fact that the unproductive activities of other regions make it harder to gain anything that way for everybody. But even if the functions ξ' and ξ'' were such that all X'' would be zero, a considerable amount of effort may be wasted in keeping such a status quo.

It is intuitively obvious that the waste of efforts upon unproductive activities could be reduced by some agreement on mutual protection between some or all of the regions. In fact, even if no explicit agreement is made, certain 'natural' constraints may prevail in the interregional market because of certain *conjectural* elements involved in the calculations of net gains from unproductive activities. If the allotment functions ξ'' have the properties indicated in (19. 7), it is clear that every region is interested in the unproductive efforts of other regions being as small as possible. If a particular region, No. i, knows, or believes, that the other regions will increase their unproductive efforts if No. i does so, the prospective gain for No. i will be smaller than in the case where such countermeasures are not expected.

Let $\hat{Y}_{ij}''$ denote the amount of unproductive effort that the region No. i assumes will be put in by region No. j *if* the region No. i should choose an amount $\hat{Y}_i''$ of such effort. Assume that, by agreement or otherwise, a set of *conjectural countermeasure functions*, ω_{ij}'', is established, e.g.

$$\hat{Y}_{ij}'' = \omega_{ij}''(\hat{Y}_i''; Y_1'', Y_2'', \ldots, Y_M''), \quad \begin{array}{l} i = 1, 2, \ldots, M, \\ j = 1, 2, \ldots, M, \end{array} \tag{19.10}$$

where the functions ω_{ij}'' are such that,

$$\hat{Y}_{ii}'' \equiv \hat{Y}_i'', \quad i = 1, 2, \ldots, M, \qquad (19.\ 10.\text{a})$$

and

$$Y_j'' \equiv \omega_{ij}''(Y_i''; Y_1'', Y_2'', \ldots, Y_M''), \quad \begin{aligned} i &= 1, 2, \ldots, M, \\ j &= 1, 2, \ldots, M. \end{aligned} \qquad (19.\ 10.\text{b})$$

The last set of identities means that if region No. i keeps a status quo (whatever it may be), the other regions are expected to do the same.

The conjectural gain for region No. i of an input $\hat{Y}_i''$ will then be

$$\hat{X}_i'' = \xi_i''(\hat{Y}_{i1}'', \hat{Y}_{i2}'', \ldots, \hat{Y}_i'', \ldots, \hat{Y}_{iiM}''; \Phi) \quad i = 1, 2, \ldots, M.$$
$$(19.\ 5.\text{b})$$

Let us assume that in these conjectural calculations each region regards the global output Φ as a *datum*, even though it may change as a result of what the various regions choose to do. And consider the 'marginal productivity' of $\hat{Y}_i''$-activity, calculated at the point $(Y_1'', Y_2'', \ldots, Y_M'')$ of actually prevailing Y''-activities. We have

$$\frac{\partial \hat{X}_i''}{\partial \hat{Y}_i''} = \sum_{j=1}^{M} \frac{\partial \xi_i''}{\partial \hat{Y}_{ij}''} \frac{\partial \omega_{ij}''}{\partial \hat{Y}_i''},$$
$$i = 1, 2, \ldots, M.$$

$\left.\begin{array}{l} \text{Calculated at the point} \\ \hat{Y}_{ij}'' = Y_j'', i = 1, 2, \ldots, M, \\ j = 1, 2, \ldots M, \text{ under the as-} \\ \text{sumption that the actual } Y''\text{-} \\ \text{values are } given \ parameters \text{ in} \\ \text{the functions } \omega''. \end{array}\right\}$ $\quad (19.\ 11)$

Suppose that the partial derivatives of the functions ω_{ij}'' with regard to the conjectural input $\hat{Y}_i''$ are all positive. And suppose that ξ_i'' has the properties (19. 7). Then all the terms in the right hand side of (19. 11) are negative, except the one for $j = i$. At a given level of Y''-inputs the conjectural marginal productivity as given by (19. 11) is therefore smaller than the 'atomistic' marginal productivity $\frac{\partial \xi_i''}{\partial Y_i''}$. Thus, if (19. 11) is the productivity that is being compared with the marginal productivity of Y'-activity, the latter may now appear more attractive.

The equilibrium conditions

$$\frac{\partial \xi_i'}{\partial Y_i'} = \frac{\partial \hat{X}_i''}{\partial \hat{Y}_i''}, \ i = 1, 2, \ldots, M, \qquad (19.\ 9.\text{a})$$

where the right hand side is given by (19.11), represent M equations between the $2M$ variables $Y'_1, Y'_2 \ldots, Y'_M$ and $Y''_1, Y''_2, \ldots, Y''_M$.

The functions ω''_{ij} could also be of such a nature that the inter-regional 'agreement' would apply only to a sub-set of regions, the 'outsiders' being assumed by everybody to act as if no agreement existed. Alternatively the functions ω''_{ij} could be such as to imply that a certain sub-set of regions would stand in solidarity against the rest. One could further try to solve the problem of whether a stable 'balance of power' would be possible by a division of the total set of regions into sub-sets of coalitions, but without any agreements between the various coalitions. But we shall not go into more detail along this line, as our main purpose has been merely to illustrate a general framework that could possibly be taken as a starting point for further studies.

Through 'unproductive' activities of competition of the kind discussed a good share of the input capacity of each region may be lost in a struggle where the net gain is zero. But as we have seen, there are obvious measures of agreement that could reduce the loss. It may be an interesting problem to deduce 'most efficient' methods of reducing the loss. On the other hand, it does not follow that such a theory of 'optimal behavior' is a good description of facts regarding the evolution of interregional relations. Some people would like to think that the world has gone — and is going — forward in this respect. Others may be more pessimistic, arguing that the scale of the struggle has increased as national organization and intra-regional unity has gained in strength. We do not claim to know the answer. What we have tried to indicate is merely that the relative position of the regions may depend essentially on the fact that the regions are in mutual contact. Our study also indicates that this contact may not necessarily lead to more uniformity in the evolution of the various regions.

We have mentioned some possible individual or joint actions with regard to the unproductive activities Y''. But we should also investigate certain possibilities of more constructive agreements and coalitions making the opportunities through productive inputs Y' more tempting in comparison with the opportunities of 'grabbing'. Such agreements or established practices have undoubtedly played an important rôle in the course of economic history. However, the effects of agreements or established practices intended to promote productive activities will depend very much upon the nature of the global production function Φ, and on the allotment functions (19. 3), and (19. 5).

Suppose e.g. that, by mutual agreement or otherwise, a set of conjectural 'response functions' has been established, stating the amount of Y'-activity each region is expected to supply *if* the other regions supply certain specified amounts. Let $\hat{Y}'_{ij}$ be the amount of productive input that the region No. i expects from region No. j *if* region No. i should choose to put in the amount $\hat{Y}'_i$. And assume that the conjectural 'response functions' are

$$\hat{Y}'_{ij} = \omega'_{ij}(\hat{Y}'_i; Y'_1, \ldots, Y'_M), \qquad \begin{array}{l} i = 1, 2, \ldots, M, \\ j = 1, 2, \ldots, M, \end{array} \qquad (19.\ 12)$$

where the functions ω'_{ij} are such that

$$\hat{Y}'_{ii} \equiv \hat{Y}'_i, \qquad i = 1, 2, \ldots, M, \qquad (19.\ 12.\text{a})$$

and

$$Y'_j \equiv \omega'_{ij}(Y'_i; Y'_1, Y'_2, \ldots, Y'_M), \qquad \begin{array}{l} i = 1, 2, \ldots, M, \\ j = 1, 2, \ldots, M. \end{array} \qquad (19.\ 12.\text{b})$$

Suppose, also, that the functions ω'_{ij} are such that

$$\frac{\partial \omega'_{ij}}{\partial \hat{Y}'_i} > 0, \qquad \begin{array}{l} i = 1, 2, \ldots, M, \\ j = 1, 2, \ldots, M. \end{array} \qquad (19.\ 13)$$

And consider the conjectural allotment functions

$$\hat{X}'_i = \xi'_i(\hat{Y}'_{i1}, \hat{Y}'_{i2}, \ldots \hat{Y}'_{ii}, \ldots, \hat{Y}'_{iM}), \qquad i = 1, 2, \ldots, M. \qquad (19.\ 3.\text{a})$$

The conjectural marginal productivities of Y'-activities, *calculated at the point* $\hat{Y}'_{ij} = Y'_j$, $i = 1, 2, \ldots, M$, $j = 1, 2, \ldots, M$, *of actually prevailing* Y'-*activities*, are given by

$$\frac{\partial \hat{X}'_i}{\partial \hat{Y}'_i} = \sum_{j=1}^{M} \frac{\partial \xi'_i}{\partial \hat{Y}'_{ij}} \frac{\partial \omega'_{ij}}{\partial \hat{Y}'_i}, \, i = 1, 2, \ldots, M, \qquad (19.\ 3.\text{b})$$

where the variables Y' in the functions ω'_{ij} *are regarded as given parameters* in the conjectural calculations.

The conjectural opportunities visualized by a region, No. i, if it changes its amount of Y'-activity, would then depend in part on whether or not the Y'-activities of the other regions compete with that of No. i. That is, the form of the allotment functions (19. 3) would indicate whether an agreement, or conjectural belief, of the form (19. 12) would be an encouragement towards more productive activities. Even if the global production function has the property that the inputs Y' are competing factors, the allotment functions (19. 3) could still be such that agreements of the type (19. 12) would mean encouragement towards increased production. The reason for this is that the factors Y' may not necessarily appear as competing in each allotment function. But it is also possible that the existence of a system of conjectural 'response functions' of the type (19. 12) may mean less global output, even if the global production function is such that the Y'-inputs are complementary, viz. if the inputs appear to be competitive factors in the allotment functions. The point is that the existence of a system of allotment functions and a global production function is not the same as saying that there is a central coordination of global production. In fact, the nature of the global production function may not be known to any of the regions or to those responsible for interregional policies. There is absolutely no reason to assume that there should be any automatic tendency towards an 'optimal' policy with regard to world output in the same sense as in a centrally directed economic unit. The decisive factors in shaping the historical interrelations between the regions may well have been conjectures regarding countermeasures, coupled with hopes for gains in a free-for-all atomistic market.

20. INTERREGIONAL CONTAGION OF EDUCATION AND KNOW-HOW

In dealing with the evolutionary system of a single region we have introduced the level of education and know-how as a variable, S. We are aware of the difficult — perhaps hopeless — task of measuring a variable of this kind and of comparing such data from different regions. We should propably look upon this variable as no more than an auxiliary parameter introduced for the purpose of deducing relations between the other, more objective, variables in the model. If we look upon the variable S in this way, the use of it may not be worse than the use of certain descriptive parameters in e.g. a demand function. Indeed, the assumed constancy of such parameters is in most cases derived from other assumptions of 'constant tastes', 'a given institutional framework', etc. Far-reaching problems of measurement may thus be hidden in the innocent-sounding statement that an elasticity of demand is approximately constant.

If we agree to use a parametric representation of the level of education and know-how in the various regions, it may be possible to construct a simplified theory concerning the educational effects of interregional contact.

Intuitively, it would seem plausible to assume that education is, in a sense, contagious. Education grows upon itself within a given region and it exercises a certain positive pressure upon the educational level of neighboring regions. But these tendencies may be only potential, the actual effect depending on the receptiveness of those 'exposed'. Here there are many possibilities. It may even be true, in some cases, that the internal growth of education in a particular direction means that the region concerned develops some sort of immunity towards impulses from abroad. It could also happen that the difference in educational level as between two regions is so large that what goes on in the advanced region has no educational value for 'beginners'. It is, in fact, quite possible that a region with an advanced educational level may learn quite a few things from a region that is generally very far behind, while the latter is not much affected by the high level of education in the former.

The receptiveness of a region to educational impulses probably depends rather strongly on the level of education already reached. It probably also depends strongly on the level of material wealth. Receptiveness may depend, in a negative direction, on the size of the population, a large population meaning more 'inertia' with regard to educational impulses. On the other hand, a large population may mean 'economies of scale' with regard to educational efforts. Whether a large population will advance more slowly or

99

more rapidly than a smaller population may depend essentially on how high the educational level already is in the regions concerned.

It is conceivable that a region may have reached a relatively high level of education and know-how, while at the same time its material facilities for utilizing available skill are scanty, perhaps because population has been growing too fast. If we consider the *rate of growth of* education and know-how, we might have two regions progressing at the same rate, but under otherwise very different conditions. One of them may e.g. have much material wealth per capita, but a relatively low educational level. The other may have a much higher educational level, but may not have the resources upon which to release fully its skill and ingenuity.

These considerations, and many others that could be added, seem to point in the direction of a formal theory that could be expressed by a system of relations,

$$\dot{S}_i = g_i(X_i, N_i, K_i, S_1, S_2, \ldots, S_M), i = 1, 2, \ldots, M. \qquad (20.1)$$

Each equation in this system can be considered as a generalization of the equation (9.4). We do not claim that the equations (20.1) are very easy to specify with regard to form, signs of derivatives etc. In addition there are — as already mentioned — some very difficult problems of measurement involved. On the other hand, the equations (20.1) could be useful in deriving explicit dynamic relations between X, N, and K, even if the system above did no more than indicate the *order* of the differential equations involved.

It is seen that equations from Sections 18 and 19, together with (20.1) and regional equations of the type (9.2) and (9.3) could form alternative, determinate, dynamic systems. That is, we could pick out alternative systems with as many relations as we have unknown functions of time. However, this may give us only a meager satisfaction if we want to arrive at explicit, verifiable theories.

From the point of view of explaining evolutionary dissimilarities the formal system (20.1) may give us some information, even if we are not able to specify the equations very explicitly. The thoughts that are formalized in (20.1) obviously mean additional possibilities of explaining relative evolutionary dissimilarities, in the same way as did the interregional relationships introduced in Sections 18 and 19.

Even if we assume that 'people are the same' in each region, it does not follow that their position in the interregional network should be the same. Such a conclusion could only be reached on the basis of some principle of 'insufficient reason', for dissimilarities or asymmetry. We have tried to show that each region may depend essentially on the activities of other regions. There has, historically, been no super-regional center of coordination guaranteeing any sort of symmetry in the relative position of the various regions. Thus, we cannot assume that the forms of the functions g_i are determined solely by the 'internal' properties of each region.

21. FRAGMENTS OF A THEORY OF MIGRATION

The causes of large migrations, such as those recorded in ancient and mediaeval history, are certainly very complex. The list of possible causes includes brutal lust for the produced riches of other regions, peaceful desire to share in the advantages of a better land, and religious and political persecution driving groups of people out of their home region. There have even been forced *immigrations*, people having been brought *into* some countries by those already there.

If we consider including migrations as an element of our theories of evolution, it is quite possible that these phenomena properly belong among the 'shocks' discussed in Part IV. On the other hand, there can be no doubt that rational and systematic economic calculations often have played an important rôle as 'pull' and 'push' factors influencing migrations. We want to limit our discussion to such factors. If we could single out these factors, we could perhaps with more confidence classify the remaining factors as random shocks.

In trying to arrive at simplified, *economic* theory of migration we have to consider, not only the economic conditions in the various regions, but also the way of economic reasoning of the prospective emigrants. What an individual moving into another region can achieve is not necessarily equal to that of the average native. The new land may be rich because of its high technological

101

level, but may not appear to offer particularly favorable opportunities to a person from a poor and illiterate region. The people of a region rich in natural resources, may live in misery for lack of technical skill, but the region may offer relatively favorable conditions to foreigners who have the know-how, even if they are relatively well off at home.

It is, indeed, quite possible to have migrations, simultaneously, in two opposite directions, people from a high-standard region moving into a low-standard region and vice versa. The important facts are what the emigrants think they can achieve in the new region when they bring with them their own level of skill and knowledge.

We shall now try to formalize these ideas.

Let n_{ij} denote the *rate* (e.g. per year) at which people from region No. j move into region No. i. Here $n_{ii} = 0$, by definition. The generalized equation (9. 2) for region No. i would then be

$$\dot{N}_i = \psi_i(X_i, N_i, K_i, S_i) + \sum_{j=1}^{M} n_{ij} - \sum_{j=1}^{M} n_{ji}, \ i = 1, 2, .., M.$$

(21. 1)

The difference between the two sums on the right hand side is the net annual immigration into region No. i.

Suppose now that it is the possibilities of production or income that count in the economic comparisons made by prospective emigrants. And suppose also, for simplicity, that the allotment functions discussed in Sections 18 and 19 are such that the total flow of goods and services, X_i, is approximately proportional to the input capacity Y_i. By appropriate choice of units we may then put $X_i = Y_i$.

The prospective emigrants from region No. j might then reason as if they were comparing their own average level of production with the average output that could be obtained in region No. i *if* that region would utilize techniques available in region No. j. Let x_{ij}^* denote the average level of output in region No. i as visualized by a prospective emigrant from region No. j. We could then write

$$x_{ij}^* = \frac{1}{N_i} \varphi_i(N_i, K_i, S_j).$$

(21. 2)

102

φ_i is the capacity function (here, by assumption, the same as the production function) of region No. i as visualized from region No. j when S_i is replaced by S_j, (while capital, K_i, and population N_i are those of region No. i).

The dynamic relations describing the 'pull' and the 'push' could then perhaps be described by a set of functions, v_{ij}, of the following type,

$$n_{ij} = v_{ij}\left(x_{ij}^*, \frac{X_j}{N_j}\right), \qquad \begin{aligned} i &= 1, 2, \ldots, M, \\ j &= 1, 2, \ldots, M. \end{aligned} \qquad (21.\,3)$$

If the functions ξ of Section 18 or 19 are more complicated than assumed here, we could perhaps assume that the per capita levels of the input capacities Y were used as a basis for comparison instead of the final outputs.

The functions v_{ij} will have to be non-negative, probably in such a way that n_{ij} is zero, identically, below a certain level of prospective economic gains. In some cases a very big positive difference between x_{ij}^* and $\frac{X_j}{N_j}$ may be required to start any migration at all. As the region No. i fills up, x_{ij}^* may fall and this may slow down the rate n_{ij}. At the same time $\frac{X_j}{N_j}$ may increase. But the effects may also work in the opposite direction. That depends on the nature of the production – or 'capacity' functions.

Even though it would seem obvious that migrations might reduce economic differences between the various regions, this conclusion is not safe. Skilled people from an 'educated' country in stagnation because of high pressure of population may move into another region that is rich but in stagnation for lack of skill. The result may be rapid economic development in the latter region. However, such effects are not adequately covered by the theory suggested in Section 20, as we did not take account of the more direct effects of migrations upon the variables S.

The relations (20. 1), (21. 1), (21. 2), (21. 3) together with regional equations of the type (9. 3) and 'productivity' relations from Sections 18 and 19 could form alternative complete dynamic systems. But, admittedly, in order to gain this level of generalization we have paid a high price in terms of direct econometric applicability of our model. On the other hand, a fairly general system, as indicated, is probably a necessary starting point for any econometric approach in the field.

VI. SOME SPECULATIONS UPON
A MORE FLEXIBLE THEORETICAL FRAMEWORK

22. RIGID DYNAMICS AND THE FREEDOM OF CHOICE

In the preceding sections we have searched for an acceptable explanation of regional economic dissimilarities. We have found possible reasons for large differences, without giving up the fundamental assumption that the various peoples of the earth are, basically, similar. Indeed, we have probably found almost too many defensible reasons! One might even feel that, in view of the multitude of causes that could lead to evolutionary differences, it is rather amazing that economic conditions in the various regions are not still more incomparable than is actually the case. And yet, the various models and theories surveyed are but crude and highly incomplete pictures of the complexity of evolutionary processes. Our dynamic models put the actions and decisions of human life into an iron frame, forcing the paths of evolution into rigid, deterministic patterns.

It is true that more flexibility is introduced by the admission of random elements. But even random processes are deterministic in the sense that the properties of the probability distributions involved must be prescribed, given in advance for all future.

The profound and noble philosophy that the human will is *really free*, that people can do, and actually do, things in an unpredictable manner, that they can change their mind to upset any forecast, — *that* philosophy has no adequate counterpart in a determinate dynamic model. It is true that in order to make an economic model complete, we may use the assumption of decisions based on free choice. We assume that the people concerned could choose between many alternatives. But they choose a particular one at any time, and the choice is assumed to be predictable! In fact, some of the most profound chapters of economic theory are devoted to demonstrating how the results of economic choice can be deduced, and that they are unique. The utility functions or

105

similar characteristics are assumed to be, so to speak, a part of the individual, something that is not chosen — it just *is*. Another assumed invariant property is that the utility functions are always maximized, subject to given constraints. The constraints are by definition not a matter of individual choice. But where then is the element of human freedom of choice in this picture?

The consequences of assuming freedom of action in the wider sense indicated are of course very clear: The assumption makes analytical economic theory futile. For the theory would lose its final goal, which is prediction. Now, it is true that not all economic facts support the view that prediction should be impossible. On the other hand, there are economic phenomena — particularly those of an evolutionary nature — that seem to defy our most vigorous efforts of forecasting. Economic theory is not entirely on the defensive. But could it not be that it has paid too little attention to the — often hazily formulated — criticism that economic theory 'deals too mechanically with the human element'? The question is to what extent economic theory could be reformed in this direction, without becoming analytically empty.

The field of long-range economic development is certainly one where there is real hope for significant findings through analytical efforts. At the same time, this field is probably one where we might do well in admitting that we cannot explain everything that has happened or is going to happen. It may be of some interest to look for possible connection between the unpredictability of certain evolutionary changes and the philosophical notion of freedom of the human mind. We want to probe a little further into this matter, while remaining within the analytical framework that we have already built up.

Consider a given region, and let N and K denote its population and its stock of capital, respectively. The term 'capital' we shall here take in a very wide sense, including all kinds of accumulated power to produce or acquire goods and services. We take it to include general education and technical know-how and all kinds of material man-made equipment and production facilities. We shall assume that N and K can be altered only gradually with time. Thus, at any given time N and K and, therefore, K/N is a *datum* for the regional population as a whole.

106

K/N being given, people can decide to work more or less intensively. They can decide to use their productive power in such a way that K will increase rapidly, or only slowly, or perhaps decrease. They can procreate at various rates, within the biological range of possibilities. They can make efforts to prolong the expectance of life, or, alternatively, even help death take a higher toll among the old and the weak. (Deliberate efforts of the latter kind are not unknown in history).

In their choice between alternatives, people are faced with a set of — in part mutually conflicting — wants and desires which reflect a *natural urge* in one direction or the other. The notion of 'free will' could then, perhaps, be introduced as an additional force that decides the rôle of the natural desires in influencing human actions.

Among the basic 'natural' propensities are probably these: 1) The desire for momentary high consumption and leisure; 2) the urge to procreate and (perhaps) to care for those alive; 3) the desire to provide for the future. (Perhaps, a fourth category should be added, viz. a general desire for action rather than a 'flat' existence).

For any one of these propensities one could point out aspects of the 'environment' (natural or man-made) that are 'favorable', others that are 'unfavorable'. There is then obviously in each case a desire for more of the former kind of 'environment', less of the latter. But these desires may be conflicting. However, the amount of 'capital', K/N, can probably be regarded as an environmental factor that is favorable from almost all angles. We shall at any rate assume that this is the case.

If N and K are defined as (differentiable) functions of time, we have

$$k(t) = \frac{d}{dt}\left(\frac{K}{N}\right) = \frac{\dot{K}}{N} - \frac{K}{N}\frac{\dot{N}}{N} \qquad (22.\ 1)$$

Here $\frac{K}{N}$ is a datum at any given point of time. But $\frac{\dot{K}}{N}$ and $\frac{\dot{N}}{N}$ are, at least in part, matters of choice. However, the meaning of the latter statement needs clarification. If it were supposed to mean that at any point of time the individuals can choose alternative values of the two 'rates', the formula (22. 1) would be nonsensical. For this formula presumes that K and N are already defined as functions of time only.

Let us introduce two quantities p and q to represent the two elements of choice mentioned, and such that

$$\frac{\dot{K}}{N} = p, \tag{22.2}$$

$$\frac{\dot{N}}{N} = q. \tag{22.3}$$

These equations have a meaning only if p and q are defined as functions of time. But we want to give meaning to the statement that p and q are (within certain bounds) free parameters of human choice.

Consider, for a moment, p and q as *constants* $p = \varkappa$, $q = \nu$. Then we have, from (22. 1),(22. 2) and (22. 3), a system of solutions that, for the sake of symmetry, can be written as

$$N = N(t, \varkappa, \nu, N_o, K_o), \tag{22.4}$$

$$K = K(t, \varkappa, \nu, N_o, K_o), \tag{22.5}$$

$$k = k(t, \varkappa, \nu, N_o, K_o). \tag{22.6}$$

If we want to study effects of changing the parameters $\varkappa$ and ν, we have to consider N, K and k as *functionals*. The equations (22. 1)–(22. 3) and their solution (22. 4)–(22. 6) become meaningless if we start talking about $\varkappa$ and ν as 'independent variables' in the functions N, K, and k, instead of as constant rates p and q.

However, suppose that, after having deduced the solutions (22. 4)–(22. 6) under the proper assumptions, we *disregard their origin* and regard N, K and k in (22. 4)–(22. 6) as *functions of* t, $\varkappa$, and ν (N_o and K_o now being regarded as constants or as functions of $\varkappa$ and ν). We then have a surface in four-dimensional space for each of the variables N, K and k. The point we now want to make is this: The functions N, K and k, each of three independent variables, as given by (22. 4)–(22. 6), would obviously satisfy equations (22. 1)–(22. 3) *if* these latter equations were interpreted as *partial differential equations*, viz.

$$\frac{\partial k}{\partial t} = \varkappa - vk \tag{22. 1.a}$$

$$\frac{\dfrac{\partial K}{\partial t}}{N} = \varkappa \tag{22. 2.a}$$

$$\frac{\dfrac{\partial N}{\partial t}}{N} = v. \tag{22. 3.a}$$

A particular solution (22. 4)–(22. 6) can now be regarded, more generally, as a means of *ordering* possible, alternative levels of N, K, and k at time t according to the hypothetical, *constant* values of p and q that would be sufficient to produce each such level. But each such level could, of course, actually be reached in infinitely many different ways, through variable time functions p and q.

This formulation brings out very clearly how essential it is in economic dynamics to be able to assume that the parameters of behavior are functions of time and that we know something about these functions. For what should we know about e.g. K at time t (or the history of K up to that time) if our 'theory' be the system (22. 1. a)–(22. 3. a)? Almost nothing. In fact, the general solution of (22. 1. a)–(22. 3. a) involves arbitrary functions and tells us very little about the functions N, K, k, unless we have additional information to be used as boundary conditions.

23. ECONOMIC HISTORY AS AN IRREVERSIBLE PROCESS OF TRIAL AND ERROR

For the sake of illustration, let us assume that the state of economic progress of a region can be described by one single characteristic, e.g. the amount of capital per head (k). We shall then have to interprete 'capital' in a very wide sense, as suggested in the previous section. The amount of capital is certainly a highly relevant variable in the theory of economic evolution, and may even be *the* best index of progress to be used for practical research restricted to a one-variable model.

We start from the partial differential equation (22. 1. a) related to a particular region. The general solution of this equation is of the form

$$k(t, \varkappa, \nu) = h(\varkappa, \nu)e^{-\nu t} + \frac{\varkappa}{\nu} \qquad (23. 1)$$

where h is an arbitrary function.

We shall assume that the parameters introduced, $\varkappa$ and ν, are restricted to a certain limited domain of practical possibilities, and that the form of h for the region concerned is fixed by certain boundary conditions. The function $k(t, \varkappa, \nu)$ is then some fixed surface in four-dimensional space.

Consider a given point on the surface $k(t, \varkappa, \nu)$, corresponding to $t = t_o$, $\varkappa = \varkappa_o$, $\nu = \nu_o$. And consider a *line* $\varkappa(t)$, $\nu(t)$ in three dimensional space $(t, \varkappa, \nu)$, defined for $t \geq t_o$ and such that $\varkappa(t_o) = \varkappa_o$, $\nu(t_o) = \nu_o$. To any such line there corresponds a path on the surface $k(t, \varkappa, \nu)$, starting at $k_o = k(t_o, \varkappa_o, \nu_o)$. Consider all possible paths of this kind obtained by assuming that $\varkappa(t)$ and $\nu(t)$ are arbitrary functions (within certain practical bounds). The bundle of paths obtained in this way may be regarded as the opportunities of choice open to a region in the position $k_o, t_o, \varkappa_o, \nu_o$.

Suppose now that the region should choose to follow a particular one of these paths *for a while* (perhaps even for a long time). Let $t_1 > t_o$ be a point of time where the region so to speak 'pauses' to reconsider whether it is satisfied with the path chosen at $t = t_o$. We may regard this as if the region has a new initial situation $k_1, t_1, \varkappa_1, \nu_1$. We may think of a new bundle of paths starting from this second initial situation, a bundle similar to the one described above. But the nature of the variable k makes it reasonable to require that each path in the new bundle of possibilities should define k as a continuous function of time at $t = t_1$.

It is now interesting to observe that the opportunities of choice at t_1 are in a sense *more restricted* than the opportunities at $t = t_o$. For not all the paths open at t_o pass through the point $k_1, t_1, \varkappa_1, \nu_1$. Similarly, at the next 'stop', say $t_2 > t_1$ there are still 'fewer' opportunities regarding paths to be chosen; and so forth. Of course, the admissible paths may not be a finite number, or even countable, so that the expression 'fewer' may be somewhat

110

problematic. Nevertheless, it is obvious that there are opportunities open at an earlier stage that are not open at a later stage.

Suppose now that at a point of time, e.g. t_n, 'much later' than e.g. t_{n-m} the regional population starts to regret very much that they did not choose another path open at t_{n-m}. It may now require enormous efforts to choose a short-cut onto that desired path. In fact, it may be deemed not worth the trouble any more.

The process that we have described is obviously irreversible. Looked upon as a process of trial and error it may, for example, gradually lead to the economic ruin of a region, or it may take the region happily along a path of rapid progress. The point is that any assumption of 'perfect foresight' in the really long run is just plain ridiculous. Neither the effects of today's action upon the state of affairs a hundred years ahead, nor the likes and dislikes of people at that later date can be foreseen with any reasonable degree of precision. People do not even think in these terms, or certainly have not often done so. Indeed, part of the current efforts of a regional population is directed towards acquiring knowledge and skills the future effects of which are not known at the time the decisions to make the efforts are taken. Thus, future tastes are not data at the time of planning. In addition, the bundle of admissible paths of development *visualized* at a given time is not exhaustive: It will depend on the 'initial position' or 'environment' at any time.

We have here outlined a dynamic process of a very general nature — too general, if we have the ambition to make long-range predictions, or to construct some rigid model explaining the past. But the analysis above may perhaps serve to support the conclusion we have previously drawn, that even small initial dissimilarities may in time cause very big — almost irreparable — gaps between potentially similar economic regions.

INDEX

113